PRACTICAL
GOURMET

Company's Coming®

Summer Entertaining

Jean Paré • Ashley Billey • James Darcy

Library and Archives Canada Cataloguing in Publication
Paré, Jean, author
    Summer entertaining / Jean Paré, Ashley Billey, James Darcy.

(Original series)
Includes index.
Co-published by: Company's Coming.
ISBN 978-1-988133-09-6 (wire-o)

    1. Seasonal cooking. 2. Cookbooks. I. Billey, Ashley, author II. Darcy, James, author III. Title. IV. Series: Paré, Jean. Original series.

TX714.P3567 2016   641.5'64   C2016-900028-1

Distributed by
Canada Book Distributors - Booklogic
11414-119 Street
Edmonton. Alberta, Canada T5G 2X6
Tel: 1-800-661-9017

We acknowledge the financial support of the Government of Canada through the Canada Book Fund for our publishing activities.

Funded by the Government of Canada
Financé par le gouvernement du Canada | Canadä

PC: 35

TABLE OF CONTENTS

Practical Gourmet

Good company and great food create a powerful combination. When laughter and conversation mix with the heady fragrance and flavours of delicious fare, we are not just sharing a meal—we are nourishing our lives. Artfully prepared dishes awaken the senses and please the palate. And here's the secret: It can all be so simple!

Company's Coming is delighted to partner with **Practical Gourmet** to introduce a new series designed to help home cooks create no-fuss, sumptuous food. It is possible to wow both the eye and the palate using readily available ingredients and minimal effort. Practical Gourmet offers sophisticated recipes without the hassle of complicated methods, special equipment or obscure ingredients.

Titles in this series feature full-page colour photos of every recipe, menu suggestions and sidebars on preparation tips and tricks.

We are excited to bring you *Summer Entertaining*, the new title in this series. Long, cold winters leave us craving the magic of summer with its warmth, sunshine and bounty of fresh fruits and vegetables. It is a time to celebrate, and what better way to enjoy summer than in the company good friends and family. Whether you are throwing an elegant garden party or a casual backyard barbecue, *Summer Entertaining* has got you covered. With recipes for every occasion, from fiestas to quiet evenings lounging on the porch, this guide captures the true essence of summer and will help make your get-togethers fun and stress-free. Guests will appreciate your thoughtfulness and skill, while you revel in how easy it was to prepare these impressive dishes. *Summer Entertaining* lets you cook and entertain in a relaxed atmosphere—and have fun doing it.

Approachable recipes, fabulous results, wonderful get-togethers—it all starts with *Summer Entertaining*.

The Jean Paré Story

Jean Paré (pronounced "jeen PAIR-ee") grew up understanding that the combination of family, friends and home cooking is the best recipe for a good life. When Jean left home, she took with her a love of cooking, many family recipes and an intriguing desire to read cookbooks as if they were novels!

When her four children had all reached school age, Jean volunteered to cater the 50th anniversary celebration of the Vermilion School of Agriculture, now Lakeland College, in Alberta, Canada. Working out of her home, Jean prepared a dinner for more than 1,000 people, launching a flourishing catering operation that continued for over 18 years.

As requests for her recipes increased, Jean was often asked the question, "Why don't you write a cookbook?" The publication of *150 Delicious Squares* on April 14, 1981 marked the debut of what would soon become one of the world's most popular cookbook series.

"Never share a recipe you wouldn't use yourself."

Company's Coming cookbooks are distributed in Canada, the United States, Australia and other world markets. Bestsellers many times over in English, Company's Coming cookbooks have also been published in French and Spanish.

Familiar and trusted in home kitchens around the world, Company's Coming cookbooks are offered in a variety of formats. Highly regarded as kitchen workbooks, the softcover Original Series, with its lay-flat plastic comb binding, is still a favourite among readers.

Jean Paré's approach to cooking has always called for quick and easy recipes using everyday ingredients. That view has served her well.

Jean continues to share what she calls The Golden Rule of Cooking: Never share a recipe you wouldn't use yourself. It's an approach that has worked— millions of times over!

Plum Perfect French Toast

Summer-ripe plums and cherries top decadent French toast, baked with cream, spices and citrus liqueur.

Large eggs	4	4
Half-and-half cream	3/4 cup	175 mL
Maple syrup	1/4 cup	60 mL
Orange liqueur	2 tbsp.	30 mL
Ground cinnamon	1/2 tsp.	2 mL
French bread slices (1 inch, 2.5 cm, thick)	6	6
Fresh plums, halved, sliced into fans (see How To, below)	6	6
Fresh cherries, pitted	1/2 cup	125 mL
Sliced fresh peaches	1/2 cup	125 mL
Granulated sugar	2 tbsp.	30 mL
Orange liqueur	2 tbsp.	30 mL

Combine first 5 ingredients in a shallow bowl.

Dip bread slices, 1 at a time, into egg mixture until coated on both sides. Arrange in a well-greased 9 x 13 inch (23 x 33 cm) pan. Pour any remaining egg mixture over bread. Bake in a 425°F (220°C) oven for 15 minutes until golden and a knife inserted in centre comes out clean.

Arrange next 3 ingredients over toast. Sprinkle with sugar and broil on top rack for 4 minutes until lightly caramelized.

Drizzle with liqueur. Serves 6.

1 serving: 250 Calories; 7 g Total Fat (2.5 g Mono, 0.5 g Poly, 3.5 g Sat); 150 mg Cholesterol; 34 g Carbohydrate (2 g Fibre, 11 g Sugar); 8 g Protein; 150 mg Sodium

HOW TO SLICE PLUMS INTO FANS

Ricotta Pancakes with Lemon Strawberries

These sweet, friendly pancakes are light and lemony, served alongside a sun-ripe strawberry, lemon and maple syrup mixture.

Lemon juice	1/4 cup	60 mL
Maple syrup	3 tbsp.	45 mL
Quartered fresh strawberries	3 cups	750 mL
Egg yolks (large)	3	3
Ricotta cheese	1 cup	250 mL
All-purpose flour	1/2 cup	125 mL
Granulated sugar	1/4 cup	60 mL
Cooking oil	2 tbsp.	30 mL
Grated lemon zest (see Tip, page 10)	1 tsp.	5 mL
Salt	1/2 tsp.	2 mL
Egg whites (large)	3	3
Cream of tartar	1/8 tsp.	0.5 mL

Combine lemon juice and maple syrup. Add strawberries and toss. Let stand for 30 minutes.

Whisk next 7 ingredients until smooth.

Beat egg whites and cream of tartar until stiff peaks form. Fold into cheese mixture. Using 1/4 cup (60 mL) batter for each pancake, cook on a greased griddle on medium for 2 to 3 minutes per side until browned. Makes about 12 pancakes. Serve with strawberry mixture. Serves 4.

1 serving: *390 Calories; 19 g Total Fat (8 g Mono, 3 g Poly, 7 g Sat); 190 mg Cholesterol; 45 g Carbohydrate (3 g Fibre, 26 g Sugar); 14 g Protein; 390 mg Sodium*

ABOUT RICOTTA

Many of us know ricotta as a cottage cheese–like substance made from cow's milk, but in Italy, ricotta comes in myriad forms, including ricotta romano, made of sheep's milk; ricotta salata, a dried, salted version similar to feta; ricotta infornata, which is baked until browned, and popular in Sicily; and ricotta affumicata, or smoked ricotta, a type enjoyed in northern Italy.

Orange-glazed Blueberry Scones

Create these tempting scones the morning after berry-picking. Glazed with citrus and filled with a luscious blueberry layer, they are the perfect accompaniment to a cup of coffee on the patio.

All-purpose flour	2 1/4 cups	550 mL
Granulated sugar	1/4 cup	60 mL
Baking powder	1 tbsp.	15 mL
Salt	1/2 tsp.	2 mL
Cold butter, cut up	1/2 cup	125 mL
Half-and-half cream	1 cup	250 mL
Grated orange zest (see Tip, below)	1/2 tsp.	2 mL
Fresh (or frozen) blueberries	3/4 cup	175 mL
Orange juice	2 tbsp.	30 mL
Butter	1 tsp.	5 mL
Icing sugar	1/2 cup	125 mL
Grated orange zest	1/4 tsp.	1 mL

Combine first 4 ingredients in a bowl. Cut butter into flour mixture until mixture resembles coarse crumbs.

Stir in cream and orange zest until just combined. Turn out onto lightly floured surface and knead gently 3 or 4 times. Divide into 2 portions. Place 1 portion onto a greased bake sheet and pat out dough to a 9 inch (23 cm) round.

Scatter blueberries over dough. Pat out remaining dough portion, place over blueberries and press down gently. Cut dough into 8 wedges and separate on bake sheet. Bake in a 400°F (200°C) oven for 30 minutes until a wooden pick inserted in centre comes out clean. Let stand for 5 minutes before transferring to a serving plate. Poke holes randomly into scone with a wooden skewer.

Microwave orange juice and butter in a small microwave-safe bowl until hot and butter is melted. Stir in icing sugar and orange zest until icing sugar is dissolved. Brush over scone and let stand for 5 minutes. Makes 8 wedges.

Tip: When a recipe calls for grated zest and juice, it's easier to grate the fruit first, then juice it. Be careful not to grate down to the pith (white part of the peel), which is bitter and best avoided.

1 wedge: *330 Calories; 16 g Total Fat (4 g Mono, 1 g Poly, 10 g Sat); 45 mg Cholesterol; 43 g Carbohydrate (1 g Fibre, 14 g Sugar); 5 g Protein; 350 mg Sodium*

Fruit Puff Pastries

Gorgeous summer-fresh fruit nestled in luxurious, citrus-kissed mascarpone atop a bed of golden puff pastry—just try to resist one.

14 oz. (397 g) package of puff pastry, thawed according to package directions	1/2	1/2
Mascarpone cheese	1 cup	250 mL
Liquid honey	2 tbsp.	30 mL
Orange juice	2 tbsp.	30 mL
Grated orange zest (see Tip, page 10)	1 tsp.	5 mL
Fresh peach slices	9	9
Fresh raspberries	9	9
Fresh strawberries, sliced	24	24

Roll out pastry on a lightly floured surface to 8 x 12 inch (20 x 30 cm) rectangle. Cut into six 4 x 4 inch (10 x 10 cm) squares. Score a 1/2 inch (12 mm) border in each square with a sharp knife. Poke centres of pastries with a fork. Bake in a 375°F (190°C) oven for 15 minutes until golden and puffed. Let stand for 10 minutes. Press down centres of pastries with a fork.

Combine next 4 ingredients and spread on pastries.

Arrange peach slices and raspberries over top on 3 pastries. Arrange strawberry slices on remaining 3 pastries. Makes 6 pastries.

1 pastry: 350 Calories; 26 g Total Fat (7 g Mono, 1.5 g Poly, 13 g Sat); 45 mg Cholesterol; 26 g Carbohydrate (2 g Fibre, 9 g Sugar); 5 g Protein; 90 mg Sodium

ABOUT MASCARPONE CHEESE

You may know mascarpone from its use as a feature ingredient in the popular dessert tiramisu. But did you know that it's technically not cheese? It's more like yogurt and is made using a similar process, by adding bacterial culture to the cream skimmed off the milk used to make Parmesan, and then heating the resulting mixture. Once it matures and thickens, it becomes a delicious "cheese."

BLT Eggs with Herb Mayonnaise

Creamy mayonnaise infused with herbs pairs with bacon and eggs, creating beloved BLT flavours with a delightfully fresh twist. A fabulous way to begin a summer day!

Mayonnaise	1/2 cup	125 mL
Chopped fresh basil	2 tbsp.	30 mL
Chopped fresh parsley	2 tbsp.	30 mL
Chopped fresh chives	1 tbsp.	15 mL
Coarsely ground pepper	1/4 tsp.	1 mL
Water	4 cups	1 L
Vinegar	2 tsp.	10 mL
Large eggs	4	4
Sourdough bread slices (1/2 inch, 12 mm) thick) toasted, cut in half	2	2
Baby lettuce leaves, lightly packed	1 cup	250 mL
Diced seeded Roma (plum) tomato	1/4 cup	60 mL
Bacon slices, cooked crisp	8	8

Combine first 5 ingredients.

Combine water and vinegar in a medium frying pan and bring to a boil. Reduce heat to medium. Break 1 egg into a shallow dish and slip into boiling water. Repeat with remaining eggs. Cook for 4 minutes until egg white is set and yolk reaches desired doneness. Remove eggs with a slotted spoon and blot dry.

Spread half of herb mayonnaise on toast and place on 4 serving plates. Arrange lettuce over toast. Place eggs on lettuce and dollop with remaining herb mayonnaise. Top with tomato and bacon. Serves 4.

1 serving: 680 Calories; 60 g Total Fat (29 g Mono, 11 g Poly, 15 g Sat); 275 mg Cholesterol; 12 g Carbohydrate (trace Fibre, 0 g Sugar); 18 g Protein; 990 mg Sodium

ABOUT SOURDOUGH BREAD

Sourdough refers to both a type of bread and a method of leavening bread. The bread is made using a special leavening agent (or starter) made from wild yeasts (as opposed to cultured yeasts) and bacteria captured from the air. This starter contains lactic and acetic acids, which produce the bread's characteristic tangy flavour. As a method of leavening bread, sourdough dates back to ancient Egypt. Once a staple food of the Gold Rush in Northern California, sourdough bread is still an important part of the food culture of San Francisco.

Smoked Cheddar Soufflés

Impressive, feather-light soufflés with luxurious smoky cheddar flavour. Your guests will think you've been up since dawn. Little will they know how simple these soufflés actually are to create.

Ingredient	Imperial	Metric
Butter, softened (see Tip, below)	2 tbsp.	30 mL
Grated Parmesan cheese	1/4 cup	60 mL
Butter	3 tbsp.	45 mL
All-purpose flour	3 tbsp.	45 mL
Milk	2/3 cup	150 mL
Grated applewood-smoked Cheddar cheese	1 cup	250 mL
Egg yolks (large)	4	4
Salt	1/4 tsp.	1 mL
Pepper	1/8 tsp.	0.5 mL
Ground nutmeg, sprinkle		
Egg whites (large)	4	4
Icing (confectioner's) sugar	2 tbsp.	30 mL
Cream of tartar	1/8 tsp.	0.5 mL

Grease eight 6 oz. (170 mL) ramekins with butter. Coat the bottom and sides with Parmesan cheese, discarding any excess.

Melt second amount of butter in a saucepan on medium. Add flour and stir for 1 minute until bubbling. Slowly add milk, stirring constantly. Cook for 1 minute until thickened. Remove from heat.

Stir in Cheddar cheese until melted. Whisk in next 4 ingredients until combined.

Beat remaining 3 ingredients until soft peaks form. Fold 1/3 of egg white mixture into cheese mixture until almost combined. Fold in remaining egg white mixture until just combined. Carefully spoon into prepared ramekins. Cover each ramekin with plastic wrap and foil. Chill overnight. Unwrap ramekins and arrange on a baking sheet. Bake in a 400°F (200°C) oven for 13 to 15 minutes until browned and centre looks dry. Serve immediately. Makes 8 soufflés.

1 soufflé: 200 Calories; 15 g Total Fat (3 g Mono, 0.5 g Poly, 9 g Sat); 135 mg Cholesterol; 15 g Carbohydrate (0 g Fibre, 3 g Sugar); 9 g Protein; 300 mg Sodium

Tip: Brushing the ramekins with softened rather than melted butter creates a slightly thicker coating, so the cheese adheres better.

Smoked Salmon on Goat Cheese Bagels

Vibrant smoked salmon, fresh spinach and goat cheese top toasted bagels for a wonderfully complex flavour combination—satisfying and sophisticated. Add some tart Granny Smith apple slices for a little extra bite or cherry tomatoes for an extra shot of colour.

Herb goat (chèvre) cheese	4 oz.	113 g
Lemon juice	2 tbsp.	30 mL
Liquid honey	2 tbsp.	30 mL
Bagels, split, toasted	4	4
Baby spinach, lightly packed	1 cup	250 mL
Smoked salmon slices	6 oz.	170 g

Stir first 3 ingredients until smooth. Spread half of mixture on bottom bagel halves.

Place bagels on serving plates and top with spinach. Drizzle with remaining cheese mixture and top with smoked salmon and bagel tops. Serves 4.

1 serving: 460 Calories; 10 g Total Fat (2 g Mono, 0.5 g Poly, 5 g Sat); 25 mg Cholesterol; 69 g Carbohydrate (3 g Fibre, 21 g Sugar); 23 g Protein; 960 mg Sodium

ABOUT SMOKED SALMON

The delicious and distinctive flavour of smoked salmon is created using one of two different methods: cold smoking, which does not cook the fish and leaves it tender and moist; or hot smoking, which cooks the fish all the way through, giving it a firmer, chewier texture.

Petit Lavender Pain au Chocolat

If stepping out to a Parisian pâtisserie isn't an option, create these delightful bundles yourself. The flakey pastries have a rich, smooth chocolate filling and fragrant lavender notes.

Whipping cream	1/3 cup	75 mL
Dried lavender	2 tsp.	10 mL
1 oz. (28 g) bittersweet chocolate baking squares , chopped	4	4
14 oz. (397 g) package of puff pastry, thawed according to package directions	1	1
Large egg	1	1
Water	1 tbsp.	15 mL
Icing (confectioners') sugar, sprinkle		

Bring whipping cream and lavender to a boil in a saucepan on medium. Remove from heat and cool. Strain through a fine mesh sieve into a microwave-safe bowl and discard solids.

Add chocolate. Microwave until chocolate is almost melted. Stir until smooth. Cool.

Roll out 1/2 (1 square) of pastry on lightly floured surface to a 9 x 12 inch (23 x 30 cm) rectangle. Cut into twelve 3 x 3 inch (7.5 x 7.5 cm) squares. Spoon about 1 tsp. (5 mL) of chocolate mixture onto edge of 1 square. Roll up tightly to enclose filling and press gently to seal. Place, seam side down, on a baking sheet lined with parchment paper. Repeat with remaining pastry.

Whisk egg and water and brush over tops of pastries. Bake in a 400°F (200°C) oven for 15 minutes until golden and puffed.

Sprinkle with icing sugar. Makes 24 pastries.

1 pastry: 130 Calories; 9 g Total Fat (4 g Mono, 1 g Poly, 3.5 g Sat); 15 mg Cholesterol; 10 g Carbohydrate (trace Fibre, 2 g Sugar); 2 g Protein; 45 mg Sodium

ABOUT LAVENDER

Lavender is a beautiful herb with a long history. Its scent has been regarded as theraputic for centuries. It has been used as an insect repellent, an ornamental plant, to scent perfume and to flavour preserves, tisanes and baked goods. Few herbs are as loved or as versatile as lavender.

Tropical Passion Smoothies

Lush, glossy smoothies to brighten the early hours. Slowly savour this blend of sweet-tart tropical flavours with an elegant note of liqueur.

Chopped frozen mango	4 cups	1 L
Passion fruit sorbet	2 cups	500 mL
Pomegranate juice	1 cup	250 mL
Orange liqueur (such as Grand Marnier)	1/4 cup	60 mL
Raspberry liqueur (such as Chambord)	1/4 cup	60 mL

Process all 5 ingredients in a blender until smooth. Serve in chilled glasses. Makes about 5 1/2 cups (1.4 L).

1/2 cup (125 mL): 260 Calories; 0 g Total Fat (0 g Mono, 0 g Poly, 0 g Sat); 0 mg Cholesterol; 54 g Carbohydrate (2 g Fibre, 52 g Sugar); 0 g Protein; 20 mg Sodium

ABOUT SORBET

Sorbet is the French word for sherbet and is typically a mix of fruit juice and water that is frozen and served as a dessert or as a palate cleanser between the courses of a meal. While sherbet can contain milk, egg whites or gelatin, sorbet does not. A sorbet is also sometimes called an ice or a granita, though its texture is often smoother than either.

Frosty Almond Café au Lait

Smooth coffee blends with lovely almond and vanilla, creating a fragrant, creamy combination to serve over ice.

Strong brewed coffee, chilled	3 cups	750 mL
French vanilla ice cream	2 cups	500 mL
Almond liqueur (such as Amaretto)	1/3 cup	75 mL

Process all 3 ingredients, in 2 batches, in a blender until smooth. Serve over ice cubes. Makes about 6 cups (1.5 L).

1 cup (250 mL): 130 Calories; 5 g Total Fat (1.5 g Mono, 0 g Poly, 3.5 g Sat); 20 mg Cholesterol; 11 g Carbohydrate (0 g Fibre, 10 g Sugar); 2 g Protein; 40 mg Sodium

ABOUT AMARETTO

Meaning "a little bitter" in Italian, amaretto is a liqueur that is often made using the kernels of apricot pits, but that tastes like almonds. The original amaretto was made in Saronno, in the north of Italy.

Al Fresco Sandwich

The simple, rustic appearance of this hearty sandwich makes way for delectably complex flavour. Soft foccacia encloses aromatic caramelized onions, Italian salami and creamy blue cheese spread—truly satisfying.

Olive oil	3 tbsp.	45 mL
Sliced onion	4 cups	1 L
Sprigs of fresh rosemary	2	2
Salt	1/4 tsp.	1 mL
Chianti wine	1/2 cup	125 mL
Baby arugula, lightly packed	4 cups	1 L
Butter, softened	1/4 cup	60 mL
Gorgonzola cheese, softened	1/4 cup	60 mL
Herb focaccia bread (10 inch, 25 cm, diameter), split horizontally	1	1
Thinly sliced deli ham	3 oz.	85 g
Thinly sliced Genoa salami	3 oz.	85 g

Heat olive oil in a large frying pan on medium. Add next 3 ingredients and cook, covered, for 10 minutes, stirring occasionally, until onion is softened. Reduce heat to medium-low and cook, uncovered, for 10 minutes, stirring occasionally, until deep golden brown (see How To, below).

Stir in wine and simmer for 5 minutes until liquid is evaporated. Remove from heat and discard rosemary sprigs.

Add arugula to onion mixture and stir until wilted.

Combine butter and cheese and spread on both halves of focaccia. Spread arugula mixture on bottom half. Arrange ham and salami over arugula mixture and cover with top half of bread. Cuts into 6 wedges.

1 wedge: 500 Calories; 25 g Total Fat (8 g Mono, 1 g Poly, 8 g Sat); 45 mg Cholesterol; 53 g Carbohydrate (3 g Fibre, 5 g Sugar); 15 g Protein; 1070 mg Sodium

HOW TO CARAMELIZE ONIONS

Cook onions, uncovered, on medium-low until deep golden brown, about 10 minutes.

Summer Vegetable Quiche

A wonderfully rich quiche chock full of summer's freshest bounty. Bake up this appetizing offering the day after a sunlit stroll through the farmers' market.

Cooking oil	2 tsp.	10 mL
Chopped fresh asparagus	2 cups	500 mL
(1 inch, 2.5 cm, pieces)		
Julienned zucchini	2/3 cup	150 mL
Julienned red pepper	1/2 cup	125 mL
Julienned yellow pepper	1/2 cup	125 mL
Shredded fresh basil	3 tbsp.	45 mL
Chopped fresh chives	2 tbsp.	30 mL
Chopped fresh dill	2 tbsp.	30 mL
Fine dry bread crumbs	2 tbsp.	30 mL
Paprika	1/2 tsp.	2 mL
Grated havarti cheese	1 cup	250 mL
Large eggs	4	4
Half-and-half cream	1 1/2 cups	375 mL
All purpose flour	2 tbsp.	30 mL
Salt	3/4 tsp.	4 mL
Pepper	1/4 tsp.	1 mL

Heat cooking oil in a frying pan on medium. Add next 4 ingredients and cook for 8 minutes until tender-crisp. Remove from heat and let stand for 15 minutes.

Stir in next 3 ingredients.

Combine bread crumbs and paprika and sprinkle mixture evenly over the bottom and sides of a greased 9 inch (23 cm) deep-dish pie plate until coated. Spoon vegetable mixture over crumbs and sprinkle with cheese.

Whisk remaining 5 ingredients together and pour over cheese. Bake on centre rack in a 375°F (190°C) oven for 45 minutes until knife inserted in centre comes out clean. Let stand on a wire rack for 15 minutes before cutting. Serve warm or at room temperature. Cuts into 8 wedges.

1 wedge: 190 Calories; 13 g Total Fat (4.5 g Mono, 1 g Poly, 7 g Sat); 135 mg Cholesterol; 8 g Carbohydrate (1 g Fibre, 2 g Sugar); 9 g Protein; 370 mg Sodium

Crispy Pecan Chicken with Shiraz Vinaigrette on Greens

Nothing says summer like luscious ripe berries and pecan-crusted chicken topping fresh greens drizzled with a Shiraz and raspberry vinaigrette. The vinaigrette can be made one day ahead and stored in refrigerator for up to 10 days in an airtight container.

Shiraz wine	1 1/2 cups	375 mL
Balsamic vinegar	3 tbsp.	45 mL
Olive oil	3 tbsp.	45 mL
Seedless raspberry jam	4 tsp.	20 mL
Large eggs	2	2
Grated Parmesan cheese	1/4 cup	60 mL
Dijon mustard	1 tbsp.	15 mL
Finely chopped pecans	1/2 cup	125 mL
Panko crumbs	1/2 cup	125 mL
Salt	1/2 tsp.	2 mL
Pepper	1/4 tsp.	1 mL
Boneless, skinless chicken breasts, cut into 1/2 inch (12 mm) slices	3	3
Cooking spray		
Large avocado, sliced	1	1
Romaine lettuce mix, lightly packed	6 cups	1.5 L
Thinly sliced cucumber	1 cup	250 mL
Fresh raspberries	1 cup	250 mL

Boil wine in a small saucepan for 10 minutes until reduced to 3/4 cup (175 mL). Chill. Transfer to a blender and add next 3 ingredients. Process until smooth and set aside.

Combine next 3 ingredients in a large bowl.

Combine next 4 ingredients in a shallow dish. Toss chicken in egg mixture and press into crumb mixture until coated. Arrange chicken on a greased wire rack set in a baking sheet and spray chicken with cooking spray. Cook in a 425°F (220°C) oven for 12 minutes until no longer pink inside.

Combine next 3 ingredients in a bowl and drizzle with 1/4 cup (60 mL) of vinaigrette. Arrange on 4 serving plates and top with chicken and raspberries. Serves 4.

1 serving: 680 Calories; 34 g Total Fat (20 g Mono, 6 g Poly, 6 g Sat); 215 mg Cholesterol; 27 g Carbohydrate (8 g Fibre, 10 g Sugar); 51 g Protein; 620 mg Sodium

Citrus Penne Radicchio Salad

This appealing pasta salad with a citrus herb dressing is perfect for a light lunch. Bright radicchio and pasta with sunny bites of orange create a deliciously diverse spectrum of flavour.

Penne pasta	2 cups	500 mL
Chopped radicchio, lightly packed	2 cups	500 mL
Chopped romaine hearts, lightly packed	2 cups	500 mL
Small orange segments, halved	2 cups	500 mL
Thinly sliced red pepper, halved	1 cup	250 mL
Orange juice	1/4 cup	60 mL
Chopped fresh basil	3 tbsp.	45 mL
Chopped fresh parsley	3 tbsp.	45 mL
Lime juice	2 tbsp.	30 mL
Liquid honey	2 tbsp.	30 mL
Olive oil	2 tbsp.	30 mL
Pink grapefruit juice	2 tbsp.	30 mL
Garlic clove, chopped	1	1
Salt	1/4 tsp.	1 mL
Grated Asiago cheese	1/2 cup	125 mL

Cook pasta in boiling salted water until tender but firm. Drain and rinse with cold water. Drain well and transfer to a large serving bowl. Add next 4 ingredients and toss.

Process next 9 ingredients in a blender until smooth. Add to pasta mixture and toss.

Sprinkle with cheese. Makes about 10 cups (2.5 L).

1 cup (250 mL): 150 Calories; 4.5 g Total Fat (2.5 g Mono, 0 g Poly, 1.5 g Sat); trace Cholesterol; 23 g Carbohydrate (2 g Fibre, 0 g Sugar); 5 g Protein; 140 mg Sodium

ABOUT RADICCHIO

Radicchio is a crisp garden green originating in the region of Veneto, in northeastern Italy. It is a variety of chicory, and shares its characteristic bitter flavour with that plant. Radicchio is usually red, but green varieties also exist. It can be eaten raw or cooked; when eaten raw in a salad, it is best mixed with sweeter ingredients to balance its sharp flavour.

Salmon and Herb Soba Salad

This uptown pasta salad is perfectly summery with a dusting of fresh herbs and sesame seeds. The pairing of tempting buckwheat noodles and moist salmon creates a light lunch to linger over. This dish can be served warm or cold.

Liquid honey	1/4 cup	60 mL
Soy sauce	1/4 cup	60 mL
Lime juice	3 tbsp.	45 mL
Sesame oil	2 tbsp.	30 mL
Chili paste (sambal oelek)	1/4 tsp.	1 mL
Pepper	1/4 tsp.	1 mL
Salmon fillet, skin removed, cut into 8 pieces	1 lb.	454 g
Soba (buckwheat noodles)	6 oz.	170 g
Chopped fresh basil	1/4 cup	60 mL
Chopped fresh parsley	1/4 cup	60 mL
Toasted sesame seeds	1/4 cup	60 mL
Chopped fresh cilantro	2 tbsp.	30 mL

Combine first 6 ingredients. Pour 1/2 cup (125 mL) mixture into a large resealable freezer bag and add salmon. Chill for 20 minutes, turning occasionally. Drain and discard marinade. Arrange salmon on a greased baking sheet lined with foil. Broil on top rack in oven for 4 minutes until fish flakes easily when tested with a fork.

Cook noodles in boiling salted water for 3 minutes until tender but firm. Drain and rinse with cold water. Drain well and add to bowl with remaining soy sauce mixture.

Combine remaining 4 ingredients. Add 2/3 of mixture to noodles and toss. Divide noodles between 4 plates and twist into a nest (see How To, below). Arrange salmon over noodles and sprinkle with remaining herb mixture. Serves 4.

1 serving: 480 Calories; 18 g Total Fat (7 g Mono, 8 g Poly, 2.5 g Sat); 60 mg Cholesterol; 52 g Carbohydrate (2 g Fibre, 16 g Sugar); 32 g Protein; 1320 mg Sodium

HOW TO TWIST SOBA NOODLES

Using a large fork (such as a carving fork), twirl the soba noodles into a nest, supporting with a spoon if needed, and arrange salmon pieces over each nest.

Chickpea Salad with Spiced Feta

A beautifully unique, Middle Eastern-inspired salad perfect for toting to your favourite picnic spot.

Lemon juice	3 tbsp.	45 mL
Olive oil	3 tbsp.	45 mL
Finely chopped shallot	2 tbsp.	30 mL
Medium sherry	1 tbsp.	15 mL
Salt	1/2 tsp.	2 mL
Pepper	1/2 tsp.	2 mL
19 oz. (540 mL) can of chickpeas (garbanzo beans), rinsed and drained	1	1
Diced tomato, optional	1 cup	250 mL
Chopped fresh parsley	1 tbsp.	15 mL
Boiling water	1 cup	250 mL
Couscous	1/2 cup	125 mL
Sliced radish	1/4 cup	60 mL
Sliced celery	1/4 cup	60 mL
Chopped fresh mint	2 tbsp.	30 mL
Grated lemon zest (see Tip, page 10)	1/4 tsp.	1 mL
Salt	1/8 tsp.	0.5 mL
Pepper	1/8 tsp.	0.5 mL
Finely crumbled feta cheese	1 cup	250 mL
Za'atar	2 tsp.	10 mL
Shredded romaine lettuce, lightly packed	2 cups	500 mL

Whisk first 6 ingredients in a bowl. Add next 3 ingredients to bowl and stir.

Pour boiling water over couscous in a heatproof bowl and stir. Let stand, covered, for 5 minutes. Fluff with a fork and cool.

Stir next 6 ingredients and chickpea mixture into couscous.

Combine cheese and za'atar in a bowl. Stir into chickpea mixture. Serves 4.

1 serving: 420 Calories; 20 g Total Fat (9 g Mono, 1 g Poly, 7 g Sat); 30 mg Cholesterol; 48 g Carbohydrate (6 g Fibre, 6 g Sugar); 16 g Protein; 1100 mg Sodium

Prosciutto Crisps with Herbed Pappardelle

A simple, rustic dish of olive oil-dressed pappardelle made colourfully inviting with herbs and baby peas. Enjoy these fresh and fabulous flavours in the garden with a glass of wine.

Chopped fresh parsley	1/3 cup	75 mL
Extra virgin olive oil	1/3 cup	75 mL
Chopped fresh basil	1/4 cup	60 mL
White balsamic vinegar	2 tbsp.	30 mL
Chopped fresh oregano	1 tbsp.	15 mL
Garlic clove, minced	1	1
Salt	1/2 tsp.	2 mL
Pappardelle pasta	3/4 lb.	340 g
Baby spinach leaves, lightly packed	4 cups	1 L
Frozen tiny peas, thawed	3 cups	750 mL
Prosciutto slices, cut into 1 inch (2.5 cm) pieces	3 1/2 oz.	100 g

Combine first 7 ingredients in a large serving bowl and let stand for 15 minutes.

Cook pasta in boiling salted water until tender but firm. Stir in spinach and peas. Drain well. Add to bowl and toss.

Arrange prosciutto on a greased wire rack set in a baking sheet. Broil on top rack in oven for 4 minutes until crisp. Add to pasta mixture and toss. Makes about 8 1/2 cups (2.1 L).

1 cup (250 mL): 160 Calories; 11 g Total Fat (7 g Mono, 0.5 g Poly, 2 g Sat); 10 mg Cholesterol; 23 g Carbohydrate (4 g Fibre, 5 g Sugar); 12 g Protein; 430 mg Sodium

ABOUT PAPPARDELLE

Pappardelle are wide egg noodles about 1 inch (2.5 cm) across, similar in style to fettucine or tagliatelle (which can be substituted in a pinch). Some are made with rippled edges, making them better for holding onto the chunky, hearty sauces these noodles are traditionally served with in their native Tuscany. Noodles with flat edges are served with thinner sauces. The name can be loosely translated as meaning to "gulp down."

Swiss Chard and Feta Galettes

Aromatic and intriguing hand-held galettes. Phyllo offers its distinctive texture, cradling a wonderful blend of earthy Swiss chard, broccoli, feta, pistachios and fresh herbs—delightfully different.

Olive oil	2 tbsp.	30 mL
Chopped sweet onion	3 cups	750 mL
Garlic cloves, minced	4	4
Chopped Swiss chard (with stems), lightly packed	10 cups	2.5 L
Broccoli, small florets	2 cups	500 mL
Large eggs, fork-beaten	3	3
Fine dry bread crumbs	1/2 cup	125 mL
Chopped fresh parsley	1/3 cup	75 mL
Chopped fresh dill	1/4 cup	60 mL
Salt	3/4 tsp.	4 mL
Coarsely ground pepper	1/2 tsp.	2 mL
Phyllo pastry sheets, thawed according to package directions	12	12
Crumbled feta cheese	1/2 cup	125 mL
Coarsely chopped pistachios, toasted	4 tsp.	20 mL

Heat olive oil in a large saucepan or Dutch oven on medium. Add onion and garlic and cook for 15 minutes until onion is browned.

Add chard and broccoli and cook for 7 minutes, stirring occasionally, until tender. Remove from heat and let stand for 20 minutes. Drain excess liquid.

Stir in next 6 ingredients until combined.

Layer 6 sheets of phyllo, lightly spraying between each layer with cooking spray. Keep remaining phyllo covered with a damp towel to prevent drying. Cut pastry stack in half crosswise. Cut each half into an 8 inch (20 cm) circle. Spread half of filling onto circles, leaving a 2 inch (5 cm) border. Sprinkle with cheese. Fold border over filling to partially enclose. Transfer to a large baking sheet. Repeat steps with remaining sheets of phyllo.

Sprinkle with pistachios and spray pastry with cooking spray. Bake in a 400°F (200°C) oven for 25 minutes until golden. Makes 4 galettes.

1/2 galette: 270 Calories; 9 g Total Fat (4 g Mono, 1 g Poly, 2.5 g Sat); 90 mg Cholesterol; 36 g Carbohydrate (4 g Fibre, 5 g Sugar); 11 g Protein; 750 mg Sodium

Steak Rice Wraps

Exotic and fresh-looking bundles of steak strips enfolded with crisp vegetables, paired with a creamy steak sauce. A light and satisfying prelude to a lazy summer lunch. Replace the steak with lettuce for vegetarian guets.

Dried crushed chilies	1/2 tsp.	2 mL
Salt	1/4 tsp.	1 mL
Pepper	1/8 tsp.	0.5 mL
Beef strip loin steak	1/2 lb.	225 g
Mayonnaise	1/2 cup	125 mL
Prepared horseradish	4 tsp.	20 mL
Finely chopped fresh chives	2 tsp.	10 mL
Rice paper rounds (6 inch, 15 cm, diameter)	12	12
Julienned cucumber (3 inches, 7.5 cm, long)	2/3 cup	150 mL
Thinly sliced red pepper	1/2 cup	125 mL
Handful of parsely leaves		
Handful of chopped chives (2 inch, 5 cm, pieces)		

Combine first 3 ingredients and sprinkle over both sides of steak. Place steak on a greased wire rack set in a baking sheet. Broil on top rack in oven for 3 minutes per side for medium or until steak reaches desired doneness. Let stand, tented with foil, for 5 minutes. Cut across the grain into thin slices.

Combine next 3 ingredients in a small bowl. Set aside.

Soak 1 rice paper round in a shallow bowl of hot water until just softened. Place on a tea towel. Arrange steak slices and some of remaining 3 ingredients across centre of round close to 1 side. Fold opposite side over filling. Roll up to enclose, leaving 1 side open and filling exposed. Arrange on a serving plate and cover with a wet towel. Repeat steps. Serve with sauce. Makes 12 wraps.

1 wrap: 150 Calories; 8 g Total Fat (4.5 g Mono, 2 g Poly, 1 g Sat); 10 mg Cholesterol; 11 g Carbohydrate (1 g Fibre, 1 g Sugar); 5 g Protein; 170 mg Sodium

ABOUT HORSERADISH

Like Swiss chard, horseradish is a plant with quite a lot of culinary and ornamental value. Usually relegated to an obscure corner of the vegetable garden and sometimes cursed for its vigorous growth, horseradish has beautiful, glossy, ornamental leaves, and pungent roots that can be peeled and grated into sauces, relishes and pickles to accompany fish or meat.

Fig Frangipane Tart

Enjoy tucking into this smooth, sweet tart with its delightfully chewy filling and the pleasing texture of tender fig seeds. Serve it up after lunch on the patio, or pack up portions for a picnic.

Pastry for 2 crust 9 inch (23 cm) pie

Butter, softened	1/4 cup	60 mL
Granulated sugar	1/3 cup	75 mL
Large egg	1	1
Almond liqueur	1 tbsp.	15 mL
Whipping cream	1 tbsp.	15 mL
Ground almonds	1/2 cup	125 mL
All-purpose flour	2 tbsp.	30 mL
Salt	1/4 tsp.	1 mL
Fresh figs, stems trimmed, quartered lengthwise	8	8
Fresh raspberries	3/4 cup	175 mL
Liquid honey, warmed	1 tbsp.	15 mL

Roll out pastry to fit an ungreased 7 1/2 x 10 1/2 inch (19 x 26 cm) rectangular tart pan with a removable bottom. Carefully lift pastry and press into bottom and up sides of pan. Trim edges.

Beat butter and sugar until light and creamy. Add next 3 ingredients and mix until smooth. Add next 3 ingredients and stir until combined. Spread onto pastry.

Arrange figs and raspberries over filling and bake on a baking sheet on bottom rack in a 375°F (190°C) oven for 40 minutes until filling is set and browned.

Brush with honey and let stand on a wire rack to cool. Cuts into 8 pieces.

1 piece: 360 Calories; 20 g Total Fat (9 g Mono, 2.5 g Poly, 7 g Sat); 40 mg Cholesterol; 42 g Carbohydrate (4 g Fibre, 23 g Sugar); 4 g Protein; 290 mg Sodium

ABOUT FRANGIPANE

Frangipane is sometimes used to name a pastry made with egg yolks, butter, flour and milk, but it usually refers to an almond-flavoured cream used as a pastry filling or topping.

Lavender Almond Cupcakes

A sweet combination of floral lavender, creamy almond butter and fresh buttermilk make these little cakes worth savouring.

Quick-cooking rolled oats	1/2 cup	125 mL
Dried lavender	2 tsp.	10 mL
All-purpose flour	1 1/2 cups	375 mL
Baking powder	1 1/2 tsp.	7 mL
Salt	1/4 tsp.	1 mL
Butter, softened	1/2 cup	125 mL
Granulated sugar	3/4 cup	175 mL
Large eggs	2	2
Buttermilk	1/2 cup	125 mL
Vanilla extract	1/2 tsp.	2 mL
Almond extract	1/4 tsp.	1 mL
Almond butter, room temperature	1/2 cup	125 mL
Butter, softened	1/2 cup	125 mL
Icing (or confectioner's) sugar	1 cup	250 mL

Process rolled oats and lavender in a blender or food processor until mixture resembles fine crumbs. Transfer to a bowl.

Add next 3 ingredients and stir.

Beat butter and sugar in a large bowl until light and fluffy. Beat in eggs, 1 at a time.

Combine next 3 ingredients. Add flour mixture in 2 additions to butter mixture, alternating with buttermilk mixture and stirring after each addition until just combined. Line 12 muffin cups with paper liners and fill 3/4 full with batter. Bake in a 350°F (175°C) oven for 20 minutes until a wooden pick inserted in centre comes out clean. Let stand in pan for 10 minutes before removing to wire racks to cool completely.

Beat almond butter and butter until combined. Add icing sugar and beat until fluffy. Pipe or spread onto cupcakes. Makes 12 cupcakes.

1 cupcake: 370 Calories; 22 g Total Fat (4.5 g Mono, 1 g Poly, 10 g Sat); 75 mg Cholesterol; 38 g Carbohydrate (2 g Fibre, 22 g Sugar); 6 g Protein; 110 mg Sodium

Minty Iced Green Tea

Nutritious green tea has never been more refreshing. Infused with mint and ginger, it's perfect for sipping as you while away the afternoon. Make pretty mint ice cubes by chopping up mint leaves and freezing them in decorative ice cube trays filled with water. Serve the tea in tall, clear, decorative glasses and add a couple of mint ice cubes to each glass.

Water	2 cups	500 mL
Liquid honey	1/2 cup	125 mL
Piece of ginger root (3 inches, 7.5 cm), sliced	1	1
Chopped fresh mint, lightly packed	1/4 cup	60 mL
Green tea bags	4	4
Water, room temperature	6 cups	1.5 L
Lemon juice	1 tbsp.	15 mL

Combine first 3 ingredients in a saucepan and bring to a boil. Stir in mint and chill.

Put teabags and water into a pitcher. Stir for 3 minutes. Chill.

Squeeze tea bags dry and discard. Strain ginger mixture into pitcher and discard solids. Stir in lemon juice. Serve over ice cubes in tall glasses. Makes about 8 cups (2 L).

1 cup (250 mL): 60 Calories; 0 g Total Fat (0 g Mono, 0 g Poly, 0 g Sat); 0 mg Cholesterol; 18 g Carbohydrate (0 g Fibre, 16 g Sugar); 0 g Protein; 0 mg Sodium

ABOUT GREEN TEA

A favourite in Asia, green tea has also become quite popular in North America. Produced from tea leaves that are steamed and dried but not fermented (as is black tea), green tea has a much lighter colour and a slightly bitter flavour said to taste more like fresh tea leaves. Green tea is believed to be beneficial to health because of its reputed antioxidant properties. You can now find its flavour added to such products as ginger ale, prepared iced tea and ice cream.

Summer Garden Steaks

Serve up a striking platter of gorgeously grilled steaks, along with the wonderfully fresh garnishes of pattypan squash, mushrooms and cherry tomatoes. Pairs well with boiled new garden potatoes that are tossed with a bit of butter, and a bottle of Pinot Noir or Zinfandel.

Sweetened orange drink crystals	3 tbsp.	45 mL
Garlic cloves, minced	4	4
Chopped fresh thyme	1 tsp	5 mL
Finely chopped fresh rosemary	1 tsp.	5 mL
Salt	1 tsp.	5 mL
Pepper	1 tsp.	5 mL
Cayenne pepper	1/8 tsp.	0.5 mL
Baby pattypan squash, halved	8	8
Fresh chanterelle mushrooms, halved if large	1 cup	250 mL
Olive oil	1 tsp.	5 mL
Olive oil	2 tsp.	10 mL
Beef tenderloin steaks (about 6 oz., 170 g, each), trimmed of fat, cut thick	4	4
Baby arugula, lightly packed	2 cups	500 mL
Cherry tomatoes	1 cup	250 mL

Combine first 7 ingredients and transfer 1 tbsp. (15 mL) mixture to a medium bowl.

Add next 3 ingredients to bowl, toss until coated and set aside.

Rub olive oil and remaining herb mixture on steaks. Cook on a greased grill on medium-high heat for 4 minutes per side for medium-rare or until steaks reach desired doneness. Let stand, tented with foil, for 10 minutes.

Cook vegetable mixture in a greased preheated barbecue wok on medium-high for 5 minutes, stirring occasionally, until squash is tender-crisp. Add arugula and tomatoes and stir for 2 minutes until greens are wilted. Arrange steaks on a serving platter and spoon vegetables over top. Serves 4.

1 serving: 380 Calories; 16 g Total Fat (7 g Mono, 1.5 g Poly, 5 g Sat); 85 mg Cholesterol; 21 g Carbohydrate (4 g Fibre, 15 g Sugar); 40 g Protein; 700 mg Sodium

ABOUT CHANTERELLE MUSHROOMS

Chanterelles are cup-shaped and grow in temperate forests around the world. They can be yellow, orange, white, brownish gray and even black, and unlike most mushrooms, they have a wrinkled underside instead of gills. Chanterelles have a light, distinctively nutty, fruity taste.

Saskatoon Stilton Bison Burgers

Thick prairie burgers of lean bison and wholesome Saskatoon berries, served with crisp, fresh condiments. A creamy hint of blue cheese takes these rustic burgers to a level of sophistication.

Finely chopped onion	1/2 cup	125 mL
Chopped frozen Saskatoon berries	1/3 cup	75 mL
Beef broth	1/4 cup	60 mL
Fine dry bread crumbs	1/4 cup	60 mL
Garlic clove, minced	1	1
Salt	1/2 tsp.	2 mL
Pepper	1/2 tsp.	2 mL
Ground bison	1 lb.	454 g
Crumbled Stilton cheese	1/3 cup	75 mL
Cooking oil	1 tbsp.	15 mL
Brioche buns	4	4

Lettuce leaves, for garnish
Tomato slices, for garnish
Pickle slices, for garnish

Combine first 7 ingredients in a bowl.

Add bison and cheese and mix until just combined (see How To, below). Shape into four 4 inch (10 cm) patties. Brush both sides of patties with cooking oil. Cook on a greased grill on medium for 5 minutes per side until internal temperature reaches 160°F (71°C).

Serve in buns with plenty of fresh condiments on the side. Makes 4 burgers.

1 burger: 650 Calories; 32 g Total Fat (10 g Mono, 2 g Poly, 12 g Sat); 110 mg Cholesterol; 55 g Carbohydrate (2 g Fibre, 8 g Sugar); 33 g Protein; 1020 mg Sodium

HOW TO MIX BISON

Don't over mix when combining your ground bison with other ingredients. Try not to squeeze or compress the meat when shaping your patties or you may end up with dry, tough burgers.

Tamarind Honey Ribs

Here are the crowd-pleasing ribs everyone will be waiting for—sticky and delicious with classic honey-garlic glaze and a tangy tamarind twist. Cold beer never tasted so good.

Baby back pork ribs (about 2 racks)	3 lbs.	1.4 kg
Salt	1 tsp.	5 mL
Pepper	1 tsp.	5 mL
Boiling water	1/2 cup	125 mL
Tamarind pulp	3 tbsp.	45 mL
Liquid honey	1/2 cup	125 mL
Soy sauce	1/4 cup	60 mL
Finely grated ginger root	2 tsp.	10 mL
Garlic cloves, minced	2	2
Chili paste (sambal oelek)	1/2 tsp.	2 mL

Sprinkle both sides of ribs with salt and pepper. Preheat gas barbecue to maintain an interior barbecue temperature of medium by leaving 1 burner unlit. Adjust burner accordingly. Place ribs, meat side down, on greased grill over unlit burner. Cook for 1 hour, turning once at halftime, until meat is tender and starting to pull away from bones.

Combine boiling water and tamarind in a heatproof bowl and let stand for 5 minutes. Press through a sieve into a saucepan and discard solids.

Stir in remaining 5 ingredients and bring to a boil. Reduce heat to medium-low and simmer, uncovered, for 10 minutes, stirring occasionally, to blend flavours. Brush ribs with honey mixture and cook for 45 minutes, turning twice and brushing with honey mixture, until ribs are glazed. Let stand, tented with foil, for 10 minutes before serving. Serves 4.

1 serving: *1100 Calories; 80 g Total Fat (36 g Mono, 7 g Poly, 30 g Sat); 275 mg Cholesterol; 39 g Carbohydrate (0 g Fibre, 35 g Sugar); 57 g Protein; 1780 mg Sodium*

ABOUT TAMARIND

The tamarind tree is native to tropical Africa and India and has seedpods that are up to 6 inches (15 cm) long and contain up to twelve seeds surrounded by fibrous pulp. The sour-sweet pulp is extracted by softening the pods in hot water and running them through a sieve to remove the fibers. Tamarind pulp is a common ingredient in Indian, Asian and Middle Eastern cuisines and is used in soups, sauces, stews, marinades, chutneys, cakes, candies, jams and beverages. It can be purchased ready-to-use in jars or blocks from ethnic markets.

Citrus Chili Chicken

This is no ordinary barbecued chicken. With an infusion of citrus flavour and a touch of lingering chili heat, these drumsticks are supremely satisfying. Serve with chilled Riesling or Sauvignon Blanc, ice-cold beer, lemonade or iced tea.

Brown sugar, packed	2 tbsp.	30 mL
Ground chipotle chili pepper	2 tsp.	10 mL
Garlic powder	1 tsp.	5 mL
Salt	3/4 tsp.	4 mL
Ground cumin	1/2 tsp.	2 mL
Chicken drumsticks (about 4 oz., 113 g, each)	12	12
Orange juice	1 cup	250 mL
Lime juice	1/4 cup	60 mL

Combine first 5 ingredients.

Rub half of brown sugar mixture over chicken and chill, covered, for 30 minutes.

Combine orange and lime juice in a small saucepan. Stir in remaining brown sugar mixture and bring to a boil. Reduce heat to medium. Gently boil, uncovered, for 20 minutes, stirring occasionally, until mixture is reduced to a syrup consistency. Reserve 3 tbsp. (45 mL). Cook chicken on a greased grill on medium for 30 to 35 minutes, turning occasionally and brushing with remaining orange juice mixture until internal temperature reaches 170°F (77°C). Brush with reserved orange juice mixture. Makes 12 drumsticks.

1 drumstick: 140 Calories; 8 g Total Fat (3 g Mono, 2 g Poly, 2 g Sat); 50 mg Cholesterol; 5 g Carbohydrate (0 g Fibre, 2 g Sugar); 12 g Protein; 200 mg Sodium

Salmon with Cucumber Basil Cream

Please partygoers with wonderfully seasoned grilled salmon, paired with a refreshing, creamy sauce of cucumber and herbs.

Grated English cucumber	1 cup	250 mL
Mascarpone cheese	1/4 cup	60 mL
Finely chopped fresh basil	1 tbsp.	15 mL
Finely chopped fresh chives	1 tbsp.	15 mL
White balsamic vinegar	2 tsp.	10 mL
Salt	1/4 tsp.	1 mL
Pepper	1/8 tsp.	0.5 mL
Basil pesto	2 tbsp.	30 mL
Salmon steaks (about 7 oz., 200 g, each)	4	4
Arugula, lightly packed	2 cups	500 mL

Combine first 7 ingredients and set aside.

Spread pesto over steaks and cook on a greased grill on medium-high for 8 minutes, flipping once, until fish flakes easily when tested with a fork.

Arrange arugula and fillets on a serving plate and serve with sauce. Serves 4.

1 serving: 340 Calories; 19 g Total Fat (3.5 g Mono, 4.5 g Poly, 6 g Sat); 115 mg Cholesterol; 3 g Carbohydrate (trace Fibre, 2 g Sugar); 36 g Protein; 300 mg Sodium

ABOUT BALSAMIC VINEGAR

Traditional balsamic is a deep brown, sweet-sour, slightly syrupy vinegar made in Italy according to ancient traditions. The most famous variety is made in Modena and is strictly regulated. In fact, by law vinegar labeled aceto balsamico tradizionale di Modena must have been wood-aged for at least twelve years. The best balsamic vinegars are made from very sweet Trebbiano grapes that go through a process of fermentation, boiling and filtering a number of times before being stored in wooden barrels to further ferment, evaporate and thicken. Balsamic vinegar is aged for a minimum of four to five years before it is sold.

Spanish-style Clams

A decadent offering for a sophisticated seafood lovers' feast—clams surrounded by sausage and gremolata, all marinating in a rich and spicy broth. Mussels would also work well in this recipe. For an attractive look, serve this dish on a large square or round platter with a big basket of bread and a green salad on the side. Providing individual-sized baguettes for each guest would be a nice touch.

Clams	4 lbs.	900 g
Chopped onion	1 cup	250 mL
Hot Italian sausage meat	1/2 lb.	225 g
Garlic cloves, minced	3	3
14 oz. (398 mL) can of diced tomatoes, drained	1	1
Dry white wine	1 cup	250 mL
Orange juice	1/4 cup	60 mL
Smoked (sweet) paprika	2 tsp.	10 mL
Pepper	1/8 tsp.	0.5 mL
Chopped fresh parsley	2 tbsp.	30 mL
Grated orange zest (see Tip, page 10)	2 tsp.	10 mL

Lightly tap any clams that are opened 1/4 inch (6 mm) or more. Discard any that do not close. Put clams into a 10 x 12 inch (25 x 30 cm) foil roasting pan.

Heat a frying pan on medium-high. Scramble-fry next 3 ingredients for 7 minutes until sausage is browned. Drain.

Add next 5 ingredients and bring to a boil. Pour over clams and cover pan tightly with foil. Place pan on an ungreased grill on high. Close lid. Cook for 20 minutes until clams are opened. Discard any that are not opened. Transfer to a large serving dish.

Combine parsley and orange zest and sprinkle over top. Serve with crusty bread. Serves 8.

1 serving: 230 Calories; 10 g Total Fat (0 g Mono, 0 g Poly, 3 g Sat); 60 mg Cholesterol; 10 g Carbohydrate (1 g Fibre, 3 g Sugar); 20 g Protein; 490 mg Sodium

Summertime Pizzas

These fun and fresh flatbread pizzas are up for grabs—slice them into thin wedges and encourage everyone to sample each combination. You won't be able to decide on a favourite.

Pita breads (7 inch, 18 cm, diameter)	4	4
Olive oil	2 tbsp.	30 mL
Lemon wedges	2	2

HALLOUMI TOMATO PIZZA

Za'atar	1 tsp.	5 mL
Grated halloumi cheese	1/4 cup	60 mL
Chopped, seeded tomato	1/4 cup	60 mL

PROSCIUTTO LEMON PIZZA

Chopped prosciutto	3 tbsp.	45 mL
Fresh figs, quartered	4	4
Grated mozzarella cheese	1/4 cup	60 mL
Coarsely ground pepper	1/8 tsp.	0.5 mL
Fresh basil leaves (add after cooking)	2 tbsp.	30 mL

SMOKED CHICKEN AND GOAT CHEESE PIZZA

Chopped smoked chicken	1/4 cup	60 mL
Crumbled goat cheese	3 tbsp.	45 mL
Dried crushed chilies	1/4 tsp.	1 mL
Diced avocado (add after cooking)	1/4 cup	60 mL

Place pitas on separate sheets of foil and brush with olive oil. Squeeze lemon over top.

To assemble each pizza, top pitas with ingredients, in order given.

Place pitas with foil on an ungreased grill on medium-high. Close lid and cook for 4 minutes until pitas are crisp. Makes 4 pizzas.

1 Halloumi Tomato Pizza: 340 Calories; 16 g Total Fat (4.5 g Mono, 1 g Poly, 1 g Sat); 0 mg Cholesterol; 30 g Carbohydrate (2 g Fibre, 3 g Sugar); 19 g Protein; 115 mg Sodium

1 Prosciutto Lemon Pizza: 510 Calories; 16 g Total Fat (5 g Mono, 1 g Poly, 5 g Sat); 40 mg Cholesterol; 77 g Carbohydrate (9 g Fibre, 44 g Sugar); 21 g Protein; 830 mg Sodium

1 Smoked Chicken and Goat Cheese Pizza: 390 Calories; 19 g Total Fat (10 g Mono, 1.5 g Poly, 6 g Sat); 45 mg Cholesterol; 31 g Carbohydrate (4 g Fibre, 3 g Sugar); 23 g Protein; 240 mg Sodium

Deluxe Grilled Baby Potatoes

Casually elegant—melt-in-your-mouth baby potatoes beautifully garnished with goat cheese, chives and smoky bacon. Pair these dressed-up potatoes with your favourite grilled meats.

Baby potatoes, larger ones halved	2 lbs.	900 g
Olive oil	1 tbsp.	15 mL
Garlic cloves, minced	2	2
Chopped fresh rosemary	1 tsp.	5 mL
Salt	1/2 tsp.	2 mL
Coarsely ground pepper	1/4 tsp.	1 mL
Soft goat (chèvre) cheese, crumbled	4 oz.	113 g
Chopped fresh chives	3 tbsp.	45 mL
Bacon slices, cooked crisp and crumbled	4	4

Cook potatoes in boiling salted water until tender but firm. Drain.

Combine next 5 ingredients. Add potatoes and toss until coated. Cook in a greased preheated barbecue wok on medium heat for 12 minutes, stirring occasionally, until lightly browned.

Transfer to a serving dish and sprinkle with remaining 3 ingredients, in order given. Makes about 5 1/2 cups (1.4 L).

1 serving: 170 Calories; 10 g Total Fat (4 g Mono, 1 g Poly, 3.5 g Sat); 15 mg Cholesterol; 15 g Carbohydrate (1 g Fibre, 0 g Sugar); 6 g Protein; 260 mg Sodium

ABOUT BABY POTATOES

Although baby potatoes are unrivalled for their sweetness and creaminess when fresh from the garden or farmer's market, mini potatoes are available any time of year thanks to companies that specialize in these tiny tubers. Some companies, one of which is based in Alberta, are devoted to growing and selling nothing but baby potatoes and are constantly seeking out new varieties, so consumers have their choice of many different kinds.

Grilled Corn with Avocado Lime Butter

And you thought corn on the cob couldn't get any more delicious. Avocado and lime add a fabulous new dimension to the beloved flavour of buttery grilled corn.

Butter, softened	1/4 cup	60 mL
Chopped avocado	2 tbsp.	30 mL
Lime juice	2 tsp.	10 mL
Grated lime zest (see Tip, page 10)	1/4 tsp.	1 mL
Cayenne pepper, sprinkle		
Salt, sprinkle		
Medium corncobs	4	4

Beat first 6 ingredients until smooth. Shape mixture into a log, about 1 inch (2.5 cm) in diameter. Chill for 1 to 2 hours until firm.

Place corncobs on 4 sheets of foil. Sprinkle each with 2 tsp. (10 mL) of water. Wrap tightly and cook on an ungreased grill on medium for 25 minutes, turning every 5 minutes, until tender. Serve with butter mixture. Serves 4.

1 serving: 190 Calories; 13 g Total Fat (3.5 g Mono, 1 g Poly, 8 g Sat); 30 mg Cholesterol; 18 g Carbohydrate (3 g Fibre, 3 g Sugar); 3 g Protein; 95 mg Sodium

ABOUT BUYING CORN

When buying fresh corn, check for discoloured or shriveled kernels, dark or dried up corn silks or dull, yellowing corn husks, all of which are signs that the corn is not fresh. Press your nail into a kernel; if milky juice squirts out, the corn is fresh. Because heat causes the sugars in corn to turn to starch more quickly, try to avoid buying corn sold outdoors on a hot day or when it has been sitting in sun for a long period of time. It's best to eat fresh corn as soon as possible after purchase.

Grilled Greens with Caper Butter Vinaigrette

Nothing is better than greens fresh from the garden. Surprise and delight guests with this colourful blend of romaine and radicchio, grilled for an unexpected smoky taste seldom found in salads. Sweet green onion and lemon freshness round out the summery flavours.

Olive oil	3 tbsp.	45 mL
Medium head of romaine lettuce, halved lengthwise, core intact (see Tip, below)	1	1
Small head of radicchio, quartered lengthwise, core intact (see Tip, below)	1	1
Green onions, trimmed	6	6
Pepper, sprinkle		
Butter	3 tbsp.	45 mL
Coarsely chopped capers	2 tbsp.	30 mL
Lemon juice	2 tbsp.	30 mL

Brush olive oil over next 3 ingredients and sprinkle generously with pepper. Cook vegetables on a greased grill on medium-high, turning once, until dark grill marks appear. Remove and discard cores from romaine and radicchio. Cut crosswise into 1/2 inch (12 mm) slices and transfer to a serving bowl. Cut green onion diagonally into 1/2 inch (12 mm) pieces. Add to bowl and toss.

Heat butter in a saucepan on medium-high until golden brown. Remove from heat and stir in capers and lemon juice. Pour over romaine mixture and toss. Serve immediately. Makes about 6 cups (1.5 L).

1 cup (250 mL): 180 Calories; 7 g Total Fat (4.5 g Mono, 1 g Poly, 1 g Sat); 0 mg Cholesterol; 8 g Carbohydrate (4 g Fibre, 3 g Sugar); 2 g Protein; 105 mg Sodium

Tip: Leave the cores on the greens while grilling them to make it easier to turn without all the leaves coming apart. Cut off the cores to slice and toss.

Strawberry Shortcake Trifle

This trifle is a rich treat featuring sun-ripened strawberries and soft, creamy textures—a sweet ending to a late-afternoon barbecue party.

Sliced fresh strawberries	4 cups	1 L
Raspberry liqueur (such as Chambord)	1/2 cup	125 mL
Grated orange zest	2 tsp.	10 mL
Whipping cream	2 cups	500 mL
Icing (confectioner's) sugar	1/2 cup	125 mL
Mascarpone cheese	1 cup	250 mL
Raspberry liqueur (such as Chambord)	1/4 cup	60 mL
10 1/2 oz. (298 g) frozen pound cake, thawed, cut crosswise into 1/4 inch (6 mm) slices	1	1
Shaved white chocolate, for garnish		

Combine first 3 ingredients in a bowl and let stand, covered, for 20 minutes.

Beat whipping cream and icing sugar until soft peaks form. Add cheese and mix well.

Pour liqueur into a shallow dish. Dip cake slices, 1 at a time, into liqueur. Spoon half of strawberry mixture into a glass serving bowl. Top with half of dipped cake slices and half of cheese mixture. Repeat layers with remaining strawberry mixture, cake slices and cheese mixture. Garnish with white chocolate. Chill, covered, for 2 to 4 hours. Serves 8.

1 serving: 520 Calories; 37 g Total Fat (8 g Mono, 1 g Poly, 23 g Sat); 185 mg Cholesterol; 33 g Carbohydrate (2 g Fibre, 11 g Sugar); 5 g Protein; 180 mg Sodium

ABOUT CHAMBORD

Chambord is a French liqueur made of raspberries and blackberries. It is still produced in an old château in the Loire Valley of France. It has a beautiful garnet colour and a unique raspberry flavour and aroma.

Tropical Punch

This refreshing punch will evoke the hot sun and cooling sea breezes of the tropics. Gorgeous star fruit and cranberries add an appetizing look and lovely colour—add rum or vodka for a party!

Mango juice, chilled	4 cups	1 L
Passion fruit juice, chilled	4 cups	1 L
Sparkling white grape juice, chilled	3 cups	750 mL
White cranberry juice, chilled	3 cups	750 mL
Crushed ice	2 cups	500 mL
Frozen cranberries	1/2 cup	125 mL
Small star fruit, cut crosswise into 1/4 inch (6 mm) thick slices	1	1

Combine all 7 ingredients in a large punch bowl. Makes about 16 cups (4 L).

1 cup (250 mL): 130 Calories; 0 g Total Fat (0 g Mono, 0 g Poly, 0 g Sat); 0 mg Cholesterol; 32 g Carbohydrate (1 g Fibre, 29 g Sugar); 0 g Protein; 15 mg Sodium

ABOUT STAR FRUIT

Also known by the name carambola, star fruit thrives in tropical climates. When cut crosswise, it has a beautiful star shape and light yellow, translucent flesh. When fully ripe, it is quite sweet and juicy, but it can also be quite tart, which makes it useful in both sweet and savoury dishes. Star fruit in good condition can be stored for up to two weeks in the refrigerator. Green star fruit can be left to ripen to a golden yellow at room temperature.

White Bean and Lobster Salad

This delicate, fresh salad pairs wonderfully with a semi-dry champagne or white wine (a Sauvignon Blanc) and crusty bread. The lobster can be served chilled or slightly warm and should be cooked in the shell for the best flavour.

19 oz. (540 mL) can of navy beans, rinsed and drained	1	1
Baby arugula, lightly packed	2 cups	500 mL
Cherry tomatoes, quartered	1 cup	250 mL
Cooking oil	2 tbsp.	30 mL
Liquid honey	1 tbsp.	15 mL
Grated orange zest	2 tsp.	10 mL
Celery salt	1/4 tsp.	1 mL
Pepper	1/8 tsp.	0.5 mL
White wine vinegar	3 tbsp.	45 mL
Saffron	1/8 tsp.	0.5 mL
Frozen lobster tails (4 oz., 113 g, each), thawed	4	4
Medium oranges, segmented	2	2
Finely chopped red pepper	1/4 cup	60 mL
Finely chopped yellow pepper	1/4 cup	60 mL
Chopped fresh chives	2 tbsp.	30 mL

Combine first 8 ingredients in a medium bowl.

Microwave vinegar in a microwave-safe bowl until warm. Stir in saffron and let stand for 5 minutes. Drizzle over bean mixture and toss. Chill, covered, for 2 hours, stirring occasionally.

Cook lobster tails in a partially covered pot of simmering, salted water for 10 minutes until lobster is opaque. Drain and cool in ice water for 5 minutes until cold. Remove and discard shells.

Transfer bean mixture to 4 serving plates. Arrange orange segments and lobster on top. Sprinkle with remaining 3 ingredients. Serves 4.

1 serving: 300 Calories; 8 g Total Fat (4 g Mono, 2 g Poly, 1 g Sat); 110 mg Cholesterol; 31 g Carbohydrate (9 g Fibre, 13 g Sugar); 26 g Protein; 590 mg Sodium

Grilled Nectarine Salad

A unique twist on summertime salad. Delight guests with this unexpected blend of Mediterranean-inspired salad and sweet grilled fruit. This dish is excellent paired with a chilled Chardonnay or Reisling.

Chopped fresh mint	1 tbsp.	15 mL
Extra virgin olive oil	1 tbsp.	15 mL
Lemon juice	1 tbsp.	15 mL
Chopped fresh oregano	2 tsp.	10 mL
Chopped fresh thyme	1 tsp.	5 mL
Liquid honey	1 tsp.	5 mL
Grated lemon zest (see Tip, page 10)	1/2 tsp.	2 mL
Coarsely ground pepper	1/4 tsp.	1 mL
Extra virgin olive oil	1 tbsp.	15 mL
Liquid honey	2 tsp.	10 mL
Nectarines, halved	3	3
Spring mix lettuce, lightly packed	4 cups	1 L
Cocktail bocconcini	2/3 cup	150 mL
Thinly sliced red onion	1/3 cup	75 mL

Combine first 8 ingredients. Chill, covered, for 30 minutes to blend flavours.

Combine olive oil and honey in a large bowl. Add nectarines and toss. Cook, cut side down, on a well-greased grill on medium for 1 to 2 minutes until grill marks appear. Slice nectarines and put into same large bowl.

Add lettuce, bocconcini, red onion and dressing. Toss. Makes about 6 cups (1.5 L).

1 cup (250 mL): 160 Calories; 10 g Total Fat (3.5 g Mono, 0 g Poly, 3.5 g Sat); 20 mg Cholesterol; 12 g Carbohydrate (2 g Fibre, 8 g Sugar); 8 g Protein; 40 mg Sodium

ABOUT NECTARINES

At their peak in July and August, nectarines are slightly firmer and more flavourful than peaches, so they are a better choice for the grill. Although once believed to be a cross between a peach and a plum, nectarines are now thought to have evolved from a type of peach as far back as 2000 years ago.

Plum, Cantaloupe and Basil Soup

A unique starter to attract guests to their seats—shallow bowls of gorgeously vibrant plum soup. Tart and fresh with a surprising blend of sweet and savoury flavours.

Lemon juice	2 tbsp.	30 mL
Finely diced shallot	1 tbsp.	15 mL
Granulated sugar	1 tbsp.	15 mL
Olive oil	1 tbsp.	15 mL
Water	1 cup	250 mL
Dry white wine	3/4 cup	175 mL
Salt	1/2 tsp.	2 mL
Black plums, halved	1/2 lb.	225 g
Whole green cardamom pods, bruised	3	3
Cantaloupe balls (1 inch, 2.5 cm, diameter)	12	12
Finely shredded fresh basil	1/4 cup	60 mL

Combine first 4 ingredients and let stand for 30 minutes.

Bring next 3 ingredients to a boil in a large saucepan. Stir in plums and cardamom and reduce heat to medium-low. Simmer, uncovered, for 30 minutes. Discard cardamom. Set mixture aside to cool. Transfer to a blender or food processor. Add lemon juice mixture and process until smooth. Chill.

Arrange cantaloupe balls in centre of 4 shallow bowls. Arrange basil between cantaloupe balls. Fill bowls about 2/3 full with soup. Serves 4.

1 serving: 130 Calories; 3.5 g Total Fat (2.5 g Mono, 0 g Poly, 0.5 g Sat); 0 mg Cholesterol; 17 g Carbohydrate (1 g Fibre, 14 g Sugar); 1 g Protein; 10 mg Sodium

Fresh Asparagus with Pernod Sabayon

There's nothing better than fresh asparagus in the summertime—except perhaps when it's beautifully paired with a delicate, liquorice-kissed sabayon sprinkled with chives. This dish pairs perfectly with grilled fish, seafood or meats.

Fresh asparagus, trimmed	2 lbs.	900 g
Egg yolks (large)	4	4
Licorice liqueur (such as Pernod)	2 tbsp.	30 mL
Dry white wine	1 tbsp.	15 mL
Lemon juice	1 tbsp.	15 mL
Salt	1/8 tsp.	0.5 mL
Cayenne pepper, to taste		
Dijon mustard (with whole seeds)	2 tsp.	10 mL
Chopped fresh chives	2 tbsp.	30 mL

Cook asparagus in boiling salted water for 4 minutes until tender-crisp. Drain and arrange on a serving plate.

Whisk next 6 ingredients in a stainless steel bowl until frothy. Set over simmering water in a large saucepan so that bottom of bowl is not touching water. Whisk for 30 to 40 seconds until mixture is thickened and fluffy. Remove from heat.

Gently whisk in mustard. Drizzle sauce over asparagus and sprinkle with chives. Serves 4.

1 serving: 120 Calories; 4.5 g Total Fat (2 g Mono, 1 g Poly, 1.5 g Sat); 210 mg Cholesterol; 10 g Carbohydrate (5 g Fibre, 5 g Sugar); 8 g Protein; 120 mg Sodium

ABOUT PERNOD

Pernod is the brand name of a type of French liqueur and apéritif known as pastis. Pastis was the successor to absinthe, a similar drink made with a toxic form of wormwood oil thought to cause brain damage and banned in France in 1915. Flavoured with anise and sugar, pastis is normally diluted with water and enjoyed as as a thirst-quencher in the summer months, especially in southeast France. It is a clear, light yellow colour until it is diluted with water, after which it becomes cloudy.

Tamarind-glazed Rack of Lamb

A succulent rack of lamb with a fresh orange drizzle, suited for casually elegant entertaining. The intense flavour combination takes you on a journey from tangy tamarind and sweet molasses to mild chili heat.

Boiling water	1/3 cup	75 mL
Tamarind pulp	2 tbsp.	30 mL
Orange juice	1/3 cup	75 mL
Fancy (mild) molasses	3 tbsp.	45 mL
Dried crushed chilies	1/2 tsp.	2 mL
Lime juice	1 tsp.	5 mL
Racks of lamb (8 ribs each)	2	2
Salt	3/4 tsp.	4 mL
Pepper	1/2 tsp.	2 mL
Cooking oil	2 tsp.	10 mL
Orange wedges	2	2

Combine boiling water and tamarind in a heatproof bowl and let stand for 5 minutes. Press through a sieve into a small saucepan and discard solids.

Stir in next 3 ingredients and bring to a boil. Reduce heat to medium-low. Simmer, uncovered, for 10 minutes, stirring occasionally, until thickened and reduced to 1/2 cup (125 mL). Remove from heat.

Stir in lime juice and reserve 1/4 cup (60 mL) sauce.

Sprinkle lamb with salt and pepper. Heat cooking oil in a large frying pan on medium-high. Add lamb, meat side down, and cook for 3 minutes until browned. Place lamb, meat side up, on a greased baking sheet. Brush remaining sauce over lamb. Cook in a 375°F (190°C) oven for 25 minutes until internal temperature reaches 145°F (63°C) for medium-rare or until lamb reaches desired doneness. Let stand, tented with foil, for 10 minutes. Cut into 1-bone portions and arrange on a serving plate. Drizzle with reserved sauce.

Squeeze orange wedges over lamb. Serves 4.

1 serving: 310 Calories; 16 g Total Fat (5 g Mono, 1 g Poly, 7 g Sat); 105 mg Cholesterol; 19 g Carbohydrate (1 g Fibre, 12 g Sugar); 27 g Protein; 550 mg Sodium

Prosciutto-wrapped Stuffed Chicken

Stir the senses with beautifully plated stuffed chicken draped with proscuitto, nestled on a bed of lightly-dressed argula with toasted pine nuts. A marvellous entrée evocative of summertime freshness.

Olive oil	2 tsp.	10 mL
Chopped onion	1 cup	250 mL
Diced zucchini	1 cup	250 mL
Chopped roasted red pepper, blotted dry	1/2 cup	125 mL
Basil pesto	1 tbsp.	15 mL
Boneless, skinless chicken breast halves (about 4 oz., 113 g, each)	4	4
Salt	1/2 tsp.	2 mL
Pepper	1/4 tsp.	1 mL
Prosciutto slices	4	4
Lemon juice	2 tbsp.	30 mL
Olive oil	2 tbsp.	30 mL
Shredded fresh basil	1 tbsp.	15 mL
Baby arugula, lightly packed	2 cups	500 mL
Thinly sliced English cucumber, cut lengthwise	1 cup	250 mL
Pine nuts, toasted	2 tbsp.	30 mL

Heat olive oil in a frying pan on medium. Add onion and cook for 8 minutes until onion is softened. Add zucchini and cook for 5 minutes until zucchini starts to soften. Stir in red pepper and pesto. Remove from heat.

Cut slits horizontally in chicken to form pockets. Stuff with zucchini mixture, secure with wooden picks and sprinkle with salt and pepper. Wrap with prosciutto slices and arrange on a greased baking sheet. Cook in a 400°F (200°C) oven for 20 to 25 minutes until internal temperature of chicken, not stuffing, reaches 170°F (77°C). Remove picks.

Combine next 3 ingredients. Add arugula and cucumber and toss. Arrange on 4 serving plates. Top with chicken and sprinkle with pine nuts. Serves 4.

1 serving: 350 Calories; 18 g Total Fat (8 g Mono, 3 g Poly, 3 g Sat); 95 mg Cholesterol; 8 g Carbohydrate (2 g Fibre, 5 g Sugar); 40 g Protein; 790 mg Sodium

Dilled Trout Parcels with Lemon Sauce

A fun yet sophisticated entrée, intriguing phyllo bundles offer the pleasing textures of steelhead and dilled vegetables. A lemon sauce drizzle perfectly ties the flavours together. Serve with a fresh tossed salad on white plates for a cool, elegant summer dinner.

Thinly sliced baby red potato	2/3 cup	150 mL
Thinly sliced carrot	2/3 cup	150 mL
Thinly sliced zucchini	2/3 cup	150 mL
Butter, melted	1 tbsp.	15 mL
Chopped fresh dill	1 tbsp.	15 mL
Salt	1/4 tsp.	1 mL
Pepper	1/8 tsp.	0.5 mL
Butter, melted	1/2 cup	125 mL
Chopped fresh dill	1 tbsp.	15 mL
Phyllo pastry sheets, thawed according to package directions	3	3
Steelhead trout fillet, skin and small bones removed, cut into 4 pieces	1 lb.	454 g
Mayonnaise	1/3 cup	75 mL
Lemon juice	1 tbsp.	15 mL
Dry white wine	1 tsp.	5 mL

Blanch first 3 ingredients separately in boiling, salted water for 1 to 2 minutes until starting to soften. Drain and cool in a bowl of ice water for 1 minute. Drain well and transfer to a bowl.

Add next 4 ingredients and toss.

Combine second amount of melted butter and dill. Brush 1 pastry sheet with some of butter mixture. Fold in half crosswise and brush with more butter mixture. Arrange 1/4 of vegetable mixture along one short edge. Place 1 fillet over vegetables. Fold long sides of pastry over fillet. Roll up from the bottom to enclose filling and place seam side down on a greased baking sheet. Repeat steps with remaining pastry sheets. Bake in a 375°F (190°C) oven for 25 minutes until golden. Transfer to serving plates.

Stir remaining 3 ingredients until smooth. Drizzle over parcels. Serves 4.

1 serving: 600 Calories; 44 g Total Fat (16 g Mono, 6 g Poly, 19 g Sat); 140 mg Cholesterol; 19 g Carbohydrate (2 g Fibre, 2 g Sugar); 27 g Protein; 440 mg Sodium

Tomato Tango Tart

This rustic tart adds a punch of fresh colour to your table. Savour the simple, rich flavours of summer topped off with fragrant basil and a drizzle of olive oil.

Pastry for 9 inch (23 cm) tart pan

Butter	2 tbsp.	30 mL
Sliced leek (white part only)	2 cups	500 mL
Chopped onion	1 cup	250 mL
Salt	1/4 tsp.	1 mL
Pepper	1/8 tsp.	0.5 mL
Large Roma (plum) tomatoes, sliced	3	3
Medium yellow tomatoes, sliced	2	2
Bocconcini, sliced	6 oz.	170 g
Extra virgin olive oil	2 tbsp.	30 mL
Fresh basil leaves, torn	6	6

Roll out pastry to fit an ungreased 9 inch (23 cm) tart pan with a removable bottom. Carefully lift pastry and press into bottom and up sides of pan. Trim edges and poke bottom with fork. Line with foil and fill halfway with pie weights or dried beans. Place on a baking sheet and bake on bottom rack in a 400°F (200°C) oven for 15 minutes. Remove weights and foil and bake for 15 minutes until golden brown.

Melt butter in a frying pan on medium-high. Add next 4 ingredients and cook, covered, for 4 minutes, stirring occasionally, until softened. Reduce heat to medium and remove lid. Cook for 3 minutes until golden and no liquid remains. Transfer to a blender or food processor and process until coarsely chopped. Spread leek mixture over pastry.

Arrange next 3 ingredients in an overlapping pattern over leek mixture.

Drizzle with olive oil and scatter basil over top. Cuts into 8 wedges.

1 wedge: 210 Calories; 15 g Total Fat (6 g Mono, 1 g Poly, 6 g Sat); 20 mg Cholesterol; 15 g Carbohydrate (2 g Fibre, 4 g Sugar); 6 g Protein; 200 mg Sodium

ABOUT BOCCONCINI

Bocconcini, or "little mouthfuls" in Italian, are a form of fresh mozzarella traditionally made from the milk of water buffalo, though they are more commonly made from cow's milk in North America. Sold packed in whey or water, bocconcini are white, rindless, soft and slightly spongy, with a delicate, sweet flavour that is a world apart from the packaged mozzarella typically found at the grocery store. Bocconcini absorb flavours well and are often served in thin slices with basil, onions and sliced tomato.

Summer Vegetable Fettucine

An intriguingly elegant pasta dish with the appealing look of creamy-coated noodles—ribbons of carrot and zucchini pair perfectly with fresh herbs and parmesan.

Small green zucchini	1	1
Small yellow zucchini	1	1
Large carrot	1	1
Small red pepper, thinly sliced	1	1
Fettuccine	1/2 lb.	225 g
Butter	1/4 cup	60 mL
Sliced red onion	1 cup	250 mL
Coarsely chopped walnuts	2/3 cup	150 mL
Garlic cloves, minced	2	2
Dried crushed chilies	1/2 tsp.	2 mL
Whipping cream	1/2 cup	125 mL
Grated lemon zest	1 tbsp.	15 mL
Grated Parmesan cheese	1/2 cup	125 mL
Chopped fresh thyme	1/4 cup	60 mL

Using a vegetable peeler, peel zucchini and carrot into long strips. Cut each strip lengthwise into 3 pieces.

Cook pasta in a large saucepan of boiling salted water until tender but firm. Add zucchini, carrot and red pepper. Stir and cook for 1 minute until tender-crisp. Drain, reserving 1/2 cup (125 mL) pasta water. Return pasta and vegetables to same pot and cover to keep warm.

Melt butter in a frying pan on medium. Add next 4 ingredients and cook for 8 minutes until onion is softened.

Stir in cream and lemon zest. Add to pasta mixture along with pasta water. Toss and transfer to a serving bowl.

Sprinkle with cheese and thyme. Serves 4.

1 serving: 570 Calories; 39 g Total Fat (9 g Mono, 10 g Poly, 17 g Sat); 75 mg Cholesterol; 44 g Carbohydrate (2 g Fibre, 5 g Sugar); 16 g Protein; 420 mg Sodium

Lemon Herb Risotto with Shrimp

Risotto is always an elegant option. This creamy version with shrimp is infused with fresh herbs and parmesan. A squeeze of fresh lemon rounds out the flavours.

Prepared vegetable broth	5 cups	1.25 L
Olive oil	1 tbsp.	15 mL
Thinly sliced leek (white part only)	1 1/2 cups	375 mL
Garlic cloves, minced	3	3
Sliced fresh oyster mushrooms	2 cups	500 mL
Arborio rice	1 1/2 cups	375 mL
Dry white wine	1/2 cup	125 mL
Frozen tiny peas, thawed	2 cups	500 mL
Cooked large shrimp (peeled and deveined)	3/4 lb.	340 g
Grated Parmesan cheese	1/2 cup	125 mL
Chopped fresh parsley	1/3 cup	75 mL
Chopped fresh basil	1/4 cup	60 mL
Lemon juice	3 tbsp.	45 mL
Pepper	1/2 tsp.	2 mL

Bring broth to a boil in a saucepan. Reduce heat to low.

Heat olive oil in a large saucepan or Dutch oven on medium. Add leek and garlic. Cook for 5 minutes until leek is softened. Add mushrooms and rice and cook for 2 minutes until mushroom starts to soften. Add wine and stir for 1 minute until liquid is evaporated. Add 1 cup (250 mL) of hot broth (see How To, below). Heat and stir until broth is almost absorbed. Repeat with remaining broth, 1 cup (250 mL) at a time, until rice is tender and creamy.

Stir in peas and shrimp until heated through. Remove from heat.

Stir in remaining 5 ingredients. Makes about 7 cups (1.75 L).

1 cup (125 mL): 310 Calories; 4.5 g Total Fat (2.5 g Mono, 0.5 g Poly, 1.5 g Sat); 100 mg Cholesterol; 43 g Carbohydrate (3 g Fibre, 2 g Sugar); 18 g Protein; 660 mg Sodium

HOW TO ADD BROTH

Use a 1 cup (250 ml) ladle to add the broth. Cook, stirring, until broth is almost absorbed before adding next ladleful.

Passata Chard with Chèvre Croutons

A sophisticated first course with character—the bold flavour of crispy goat cheese croutons rounds out earthy chard and sweet tomatoes. The chèvre croutons can be prepared up to one day in advance. Keep them refrigerated until ready to cook.

Goat (chèvre) cheese	4 oz.	113 g
Large egg, fork-beaten	1	1
Panko crumbs	1 cup	250 mL
Olive oil	2 tsp.	10 mL
Olive oil	1 tsp.	5 mL
Chopped rainbow chard (with stems), lightly packed	15 cups	3.75 L
Chopped seeded yellow tomato	2 cups	500 mL
Passata	1/2 cup	125 mL
Chopped fresh basil	2 tbsp.	30 mL
White balsamic vinegar	1 tbsp.	15 mL
Garlic clove, minced	1	1
Salt	1/4 tsp.	1 mL
Coarsely ground pepper	1/4 tsp.	1 mL

Divide cheese into 8 portions and form into patties about 1 1/2 inches (3.8 cm) in diameter. Dip into egg and press into panko crumbs until coated. Repeat steps to coat cheese again. Chill for 30 minutes until firm.

Heat first amount of olive oil in a large frying pan on medium-high. Add cheese and cook for 1 minute per side until lightly browned and cheese starts to soften. Transfer to a plate and cover to keep warm.

Add remaining olive oil to same pan and reduce heat to medium. Add chard and stir. Cook, covered, for 5 minutes until chard starts to wilt. Remove from heat and drain. Stir in tomato.

Combine next 6 ingredients and add to chard mixture. Toss and transfer to 4 serving plates. Top with cheese croutons. Serves 4.

1 serving: 220 Calories; 11 g Total Fat (4.5 g Mono, 1 g Poly, 5 g Sat); 65 mg Cholesterol; 21 g Carbohydrate (4 g Fibre, 3 g Sugar); 12 g Protein; 710 mg Sodium

ABOUT PASSATA

Passata is made from uncooked, unseasoned ripe tomatoes that have been puréed and sieved to remove the skin and seeds, giving it an unadulterated tomato flavour. It's sold in jars and can be smooth or chunky depending on the level of sieving. It is useful in soups, sauces, pasta dishes, casseroles or anything that needs a concentrated tomato flavour. In a pinch, canned plain tomato sauce can be substituted for passata, but because tomato sauce usually contains salt, you will have to adjust the salt in the recipe.

Fluffy Coconut Layer Cake

This gorgeous all-white cake will be the star of the show with its understated elegance. The fluffy frosting is light and sweet with coconut ribbons, the filling creamy with lemon freshness. Chill the cake after the custard is added to make sure the layers do not slide around when the icing is applied.

Box of white cake mix (2 layer size)	1	1
Cream cheese, softened	8 oz.	250 g
11 oz. (300 mL) can of sweetened condensed milk	1	1
Lemon juice	1/3 cup	75 mL
Grated lemon zest (see Tip, page 10)	1 tbsp.	15 mL
Icing (confectioner's) sugar	2 cups	500 mL
Butter, softened	1/2 cup	125 mL
Milk	2 tbsp.	30 mL
Coconut extract	1/2 tsp.	2 mL
Unsweetened ribbon coconut	2 1/4 cups	550 mL
Lime slices	10	10

Line bottoms of three 8 inch (20 cm) round cake pans with parchment paper. Prepare cake mix according to package instructions and pour into prepared pans. Bake in a 350°F (175°C) oven for 24 minutes until a wooden pick inserted in centre of a cake comes out clean. Let stand for 10 minutes before removing to wire racks to cool completely. Trim tops of cakes to level.

Beat cream cheese in a bowl until smooth. Slowly add condensed milk, beating constantly until combined. Add lemon juice and zest and beat until smooth. Place 1 cake layer on a serving plate and spread with half of custard. Place second cake layer on top. Spread with remaining custard and top with third cake layer. Chill for 1 hour.

Beat next 4 ingredients in a mixing bowl on low until combined. Beat on high until light and fluffy. Spread over top and side of cake. Pipe 20 icing rounds on top of cake.

Lightly press coconut into icing around side of cake and on icing rounds. Garnish with lime slices. Cuts into 10 wedges.

1 wedge: 550 Calories; 29 g Total Fat (5 g Mono, 2.5 g Poly, 19 g Sat); 30 mg Cholesterol; 68 g Carbohydrate (4 g Fibre, 52 g Sugar); 7 g Protein; 510 mg Sodium

Summer Tartlets

These beautiful tartlets look as though they were made in a fancy pastry shop. With the delightful combination of fresh raspberries, mint and silky pastry cream, these little pastries taste every bit as good as they look. They will be the highlight of any summertime table.

Milk	1/2 cup	125 mL
Egg yolks, large	2	2
Granulated sugar	1 1/2 tbsp.	22 mL
Vanilla extract	2 tsp.	10 mL
All purpose flour, sifted	1 tbsp.	15 mL
Frozen mini tart shells	24	24
Fresh raspberries	48	48
Fresh mint leaves	24	24

In a saucepan, heat milk gently until hot but not bubbling. In a medium bowl, whisk egg yolks, sugar and vanilla. Add flour and whisk until well combined. Add mixture to hot milk, whisking constantly and making sure there are no lumps. Increase heat to medium, whisking constantly until thick, about 5 minutes. Remove from heat and pour into a clean bowl. Cover with plastic wrap, making sure wrap touches surface of pastry cream so no film forms, and set aside until cold, about 1 hour.

Arrange tart shells on 2 baking sheets with sides. Bake on separate racks in 375ºF (190ºC) oven for about 15 minutes, switching position of baking sheets at half time, until golden. Cool for about 15 minutes.

Spoon pastry cream into a piping bag fitted with a large star tip. Pipe cream into tart shells. Top each tartlet with two raspberries and a mint leaf. Makes 24 tartlets.

1 tartlet: 80 Calories; 4 g Total Fat (1.5 g Mono, 0.5 g Poly, 1.5 g Sat); 20 mg Cholesterol; 8 g Carbohydrate (0 g Fibre, 1 g Sugar); trace Protein; 45 mg Sodium

Garden Party Sangria

Imagine glasses of sweet sangria in the hand of every guest, candlelight illuminating the rich reds and greens of summer's ripest fruit. Chill the sangria before serving to allow the flavours to blend. A quicker version can be made using chilled wine and ginger ale, but the flavours may be less intense. White Zinfandel would make for a sweeter version of this upscale punch. Feel free to add whatever fresh fruit you have on hand.

White rum	1/4 cup	60 mL
Granulated sugar	2 tbsp.	30 mL
Orange juice	2 tbsp.	30 mL
Red and green grapes, larger ones halved	1 cup	250 mL
Sliced fresh strawberries	1 cup	250 mL
Ornage, thinly sliced	1	1
Ginger ale, chilled	4 cups	1 L
26 oz. (750 mL) bottle of rosé wine, chilled	1	1
Fresh raspberries	1 cup	250 mL
Ice cubes	12	12

Stir first 3 ingredients in a large bowl until sugar is dissolved. Add grapes and strawberries. Stir and let stand, covered, for 1 hour.

Stir in ginger ale and wine and chill for 2 hours until cold.

Add raspberries and ice cubes. Stir gently. Makes about 10 cups (2.5 L).

1 cup (250 mL): *110 Calories; 0 g Total Fat (0 g Mono, 0 g Poly, 0 g Sat); 0 mg Cholesterol; 12 g Carbohydrate (1 g Fibre, 9 g Sugar); 0 g Protein; 5 mg Sodium*

ABOUT ROSÉ WINE

Most rosé wines are made from red grapes, but the skins and stems are removed after just a couple of days. This brief contact imparts a light pink colour to these wines, but almost no tannins, so they have a light-bodied flavour and sometimes also a slight sweetness. Rosé wines are sometimes referred to as summer wines because their crispness and lightness make them very refreshing in hot weather. They pair well with light-flavoured food and should be served chilled.

Summer Spinach Bundles

Delicious things come in small, golden packages. These appealing phyllo bundles are filled with big Mediterranean flavours of spinach, lentils and feta, complete with bright lemon notes.

Bacon slices, chopped	2	2
Finely chopped onion	1/4 cup	60 mL
Baby spinach, lightly packed	1 cup	250 mL
Canned lentils, rinsed and drained	1 cup	250 mL
Crumbled feta cheese	1/2 cup	125 mL
Chopped fresh basil	1/4 cup	60 mL
Lemon juice	1 tbsp.	15 mL
Grated lemon zest (see Tip, page 10)	1 tsp.	5 mL
Pepper	1/8 tsp.	0.5 mL
Grated nutmeg, sprinkle		
Phyllo pastry sheets, thawed according to package directions	6	6
Butter, melted	1/2 cup	125 mL
Za'atar	1 tbsp.	15 mL

Cook bacon in a frying pan on medium-high until crisp. Transfer to a plate lined with paper towel to drain. Discard all but 1 tsp. (5 mL) drippings from pan. Add onion and cook for 5 minutes until softened.

Add spinach and lentils, stirring until spinach is wilted and no moisture remains. Remove from heat.

Stir in next 6 ingredients and bacon. Chill, covered.

Layer 3 sheets of phyllo, lightly brushing each layer with melted butter. Keep remaining phyllo covered with a damp towel to prevent drying. Cut pastry stack into 12 squares. Place 1 tbsp. (15 mL) filling in the centre of each pastry square. Bring the corners together, pinching just above filling and twisting slightly to create a bundle. Place on a greased baking sheet. Repeat steps. Bake in a 375°F (190°C) oven for 15 minutes until golden and filling is hot. Brush bundles with remaining butter and sprinkle with za'atar. Makes 24 bundles.

1 bundle: 90 Calories; 6 g Total Fat (2 g Mono, 0 g Poly, 3.5 g Sat); 15 mg Cholesterol; 6 g Carbohydrate (trace Fibre, trace Sugar); 2 g Protein; 140 mg Sodium

ABOUT ZA'ATAR
Za'atar is a Middle Eastern spice blend of dried thyme, dried sumac, dried marjoram and sesame seeds.

Avocado Cream Crostini

These colourful canapés are simple yet elegant—perfect for pairing with cocktails. Silky avocado cream creates a luxurious bed for smoked salmon and jalapeño.

Small avocado, chopped	1	1
Plain Balkan-style yogurt	3 tbsp.	45 mL
Sour cream	3 tbsp.	45 mL
Lemon juice	1 tbsp.	15 mL
Grated lemon zest (see Tip, page 10)	1/2 tsp.	2 mL
Salt	1/8 tsp.	0.5 mL
Melba toast rounds	24	24
Finely chopped smoked salmon	1/3 cup	75 mL
Thin slices of small jalapeño pepper (see Tip, page 146)	24	24

Process first 6 ingredients in a blender or food processor until smooth.

Spoon onto melba toasts and top with smoked salmon and jalapeño pepper. Makes 24 crostini.

1 crostini: 35 Calories; 2 g Total Fat (1 g Mono, 0 g Poly, 0 g Sat); 0 mg Cholesterol; 4 g Carbohydrate (1 g Fibre, 0 g Sugar); 1 g Protein; 55 mg Sodium

ABOUT BALKAN-STYLE YOGURT

The term "Balkan-style" refers to a specific processing method in which yogurt is set in individual cups rather than made in large vats. Some consider this type of yogurt to be creamier and more flavourful than other types. Tribes living in what today is the Balkan area of Europe are thought to have been the first to make yogurt this way, as a means of preserving milk.

Stilton and Fig Crostini

Delicate fresh figs top creamy pesto and blue cheese in these sweet and savoury bites—an elegant, gourmet look with minimal effort.

Fresh figs, stems trimmed	6	6
Baguette bread slices, cut diagonally, 1/4 inch (6 mm) thick	24	24
Arugula, lightly packed	4 cups	1 L
Pine nuts, toasted	1/3 cup	75 mL
Extra virgin olive oil	2 tbsp.	30 mL
White balsamic vinegar	2 tbsp.	30 mL
Liquid honey	1 tsp.	5 mL
Stilton cheese, crumbled	1/2 cup	125 mL

Cut each fig lengthwise into 8 wedges.

Arrange baguette slices on a greased baking sheet and broil on top rack in oven for 1 minute per side until golden and crisp.

Process next 5 ingredients in a food processor until smooth.

Spread arugula mixture on toasts and sprinkle with cheese. Broil for 1 minute until cheese is melted. Top with figs. Makes 24 crostini.

1 crostini: 70 Calories; 3.5 g Total Fat (1.5 g Mono, 1 g Poly, 1 g Sat); trace Cholesterol; 8 g Carbohydrate (1 g Fibre, 3 g Sugar); 2 g Protein; 85 mg Sodium

ABOUT STILTON CHEESE

Considered by many to be the king of English cheeses, Stilton has a rich, creamy texture and tastes like a mild Cheddar crossed with a blue cheese. It must be aged from four to six months before being eaten or it can be bitter and dry.

Lamb Slippers

Fresh and inviting, these mini-pita pockets cradle dainty lamb burgers accented with parsley and tangy yogurt sauce—satisfying Middle-Eastern flavours in a small bite.

Plain Balkan-style yogurt	1 cup	250 mL
Chopped fresh mint	1/4 cup	60 mL
Grated lemon zest	1/2 tsp.	2 mL
Salt	1/4 tsp.	1 mL
Pepper	1/4 tsp.	1 mL
Fine dry bread crumbs	2 tbsp.	30 mL
Chopped fresh mint	1/4 cup	60 mL
Chopped fresh oregano	1 tbsp.	15 mL
Garlic cloves, minced	2	2
Salt	3/4 tsp.	4 mL
Ground cinnamon	1/2 tsp.	2 mL
Ground coriander	1/2 tsp.	2 mL
Ground cumin	1/2 tsp.	2 mL
Cayenne pepper	1/8 tsp.	0.5 mL
Ground lamb	1 lb.	454 g
Pita breads (3 inch, 7.5 cm, diameter)	16	16
Coarsely chopped fresh parsley, lightly packed	1 cup	250 mL

Combine first 5 ingredients and chill until needed.

Combine next 9 ingredients.

Add lamb and mix well. Shape into 16 patties about 2 inches (5 cm) in diameter. Arrange on a greased baking sheet and cook in a 400°F (200°C) oven for 8 minutes until internal temperature reaches 160°F (71°C).

Remove top thirds of pita breads and slide patties inside. Spoon yogurt mixture and parsley onto patties. Makes 16 slippers.

1 slipper: *160 Calories; 5 g Total Fat (0 g Mono, 0 g Poly, 3 g Sat); 25 mg Cholesterol; 19 g Carbohydrate (1 g Fibre, 1 g Sugar); 8 g Protein; 340 mg Sodium:*

Devilled Quail Croustades with Chive Cream

Sophisticated croustade cups are a sight to behold—the flavour combination of tiny quail eggs, chive-infused cream and elegant caviar is simply enchanting. Use a wet knife to cut the eggs so you have clean edges.

Quail eggs, room temperature	12	12
Sour cream	1/2 cup	125 mL
Finely chopped fresh chives	1 tbsp.	15 mL
Creamed horseradish	1 tsp.	5 mL
Croustade cups (such as Siljans)	24	24
Black caviar	1 tbsp.	15 mL

Cover eggs with cold water in a saucepan and bring to a boil. Reduce heat to medium and simmer for 3 minutes. Drain and cool under cold water. Carefully peel eggs. Cut in half lengthwise with a wet knife.

Combine next 3 ingredients and spoon into a freezer bag with a corner snipped off. Pipe half of sour cream mixture into croustade cups. Place 1 egg half on each. Top with remaining sour cream mixture.

Place 1/8 tsp. (0.5 mL) caviar on each croustade. Makes 24 croustades.

1 croustade: 30 Calories; 2 g Total Fat (0.5 g Mono, 0 g Poly, 1 g Sat); 45 mg Cholesterol; 1 g Carbohydrate (0 g Fibre, 0 g Sugar); 1 g Protein; 50 mg Sodium

Rosemary and Blue Cheese Twists

Crisp and buttery pastry is twisted with sharp, aromatic blue cheese while fresh rosemary contributes subtle flavour. You can use your favourite cheese in place of the blue cheese, if you prefer, though soft cheeses such as brie won't work as well.

14 oz. (397 g) package of puff pastry, thawed according to package directions	1/2	1/2
Large egg	1	1
Water	1 tbsp.	15 mL
Finely crumbled blue cheese	1/4 cup	60 mL
Finely chopped fresh rosemary	4 tsp.	20 mL
Grated lemon zest	2 tsp.	10 mL
Pepper	1 tsp.	5 mL

Roll out pastry on a lightly floured surface to a 10 x 12 inch (25 x 30 cm) rectangle with long edge closest to you.

Combine egg and water and brush over pastry.

Combine remaining 4 ingredients and sprinkle over the bottom half of pastry. Fold top half over and gently roll with a rolling pin to seal. Cut crosswise into 24 strips, about 1/2 inch (12 mm) wide. Twist each strip, arrange about 1 inch (2.5 cm) apart on sheets lined with parchment paper and press down ends. Brush with remaining egg mixture. Bake in a 400°F (200°C) oven for 12 minutes until golden and puffed. Let stand for 5 minutes. Makes 24 cheese twists.

1 cheese twist: 50 Calories; 4 g Total Fat (2 g Mono, 0 g Poly, 1 g Sat); 10 mg Cholesterol; 4 g Carbohydrate (0 g Fibre, 0 g Sugar); 1 g Protein; 45 mg Sodium

Macadamia Chicken with Balsamic Orange Drizzle

Striking skewers to pique everyone's appetites—a unique combination of juicy orange, vibrant radicchio, chicken with nutty crunch and bright, citrus flavours.

Orange juice	1 cup	250 mL
Liquid honey	1 tbsp.	15 mL
White balsamic vinegar	1 tbsp.	15 mL
Mayonnaise	3 tbsp.	45 mL
Plain yogurt	3 tbsp.	45 mL
Liquid honey	1 tsp.	5 mL
Grated orange zest (see Tip, page 10)	1 tsp.	5 mL
Boneless, skinless chicken breast halves (about 4 oz., 113 g, each), cut into 1 inch (2.5 cm) pieces	2	2
All-purpose flour	1/4 cup	60 mL
Finely chopped salted macadamia nuts	1 cup	250 mL
Cooking spray		
Radicchio leaves, cut into 1 inch (2.5 cm) strips	3	3
Small orange segments	16	16
Bamboo skewers (6 inches, 15 cm, each)	16	16

Bring first 3 ingredients to a boil in a small saucepan, stirring occasionally. Reduce heat to medium and gently boil for 15 minutes until thickened to a syrup consistency. Cool.

Combine next 4 ingredients in a bowl.

Toss chicken in flour and roll each piece in mayonnaise mixture. Press into macadamia nuts until coated. Arrange on a greased baking sheet and spray chicken with cooking spray. Cook in a 450°F (230°C) oven for 5 minutes until no longer pink inside.

Thread chicken, radicchio and orange segments, in order given, on skewers. Arrange on a serving plate and drizzle with orange juice mixture. Makes 16 skewers.

1 skewer: 120 Calories; 9 g Total Fat (6 g Mono, 1 g Poly, 1.5 g Sat); 10 mg Cholesterol; 7 g Carbohydrate (1 g Fibre, 3 g Sugar); 5 g Protein; 30 mg Sodium

ABOUT MACADAMIA NUTS

The macadamia tree is native to Australia and was at first grown only as an ornamental. It is now grown for its nuts in California and Hawaii, the latter being where many people have encountered them. A high fat content gives the nuts a buttery flavour but also causes them to spoil quickly, so they should be stored in the refrigerator or freezer.

Shrimp and Herbed Ricotta Cups

Crisp prosciutto cups filled with creamy ricotta and fresh herbs, topped with shrimp—an irresistible appetizer for your guests, glasses of Pinot Grigio in hand.

Large egg, fork-beaten	1	1
Ricotta cheese	1 cup	250 mL
Grated Asiago cheese	2 tbsp.	30 mL
Chopped fresh basil	1 tsp.	5 mL
Chopped fresh chives	1 tsp.	5 mL
Grated lemon zest	1 tsp.	5 mL
Coarsely ground pepper	1/8 tsp.	0.5 mL
Prosciutto slices, cut into 2 1/2 inch (6.4 cm) squares	3 1/2 oz.	100 g
Uncooked small shrimp, peeled and deveined	12	12

Combine first 7 ingredients.

Line 12 greased mini-muffin cups with prosciutto (see How To, below). Fill with ricotta mixture.

Place shrimp over ricotta mixture and press down lightly. Cook in a 350°F (175°C) oven for 17 minutes until filling is set and shrimp turn pink. Serve with a squeeze of lemon. Makes 12 ricotta cups.

1 ricotta cup: 70 Calories; 4.5 g Total Fat (1 g Mono, 6 g Poly, 2.5 g Sat); 40 mg Cholesterol; trace Carbohydrate (0 g Fibre, 0 g Sugar); 6 g Protein; 200 mg Sodium

ABOUT PROSCIUTTO

Prosciutto is a type of Italian ham that has been dry-cured with salt and aged until it is no longer raw. True prosciutto is safe to eat without cooking it first because of this curing process. In Italian, this dry-cured ham is called prosciutto crudo to differentiate it from prosciutto cotto, which is ham cooked by boiling it—what North Americans would know as cooked ham. The most renowned prosciuttos come from northern Italy, such as those from Tuscany, Parma and Friuli-Venezia Giulia (San Daniele).

HOW TO LINE MUFFIN CUPS

Cut prosciutto into squares. Line muffin cups with prosciutto.

Grilled Mango Cheese Bites

The sophisticated look of these mini cocktail sandwiches makes a statement but the pairing of earthy goat cheese with sweet mango chutney and cilantro steals the show.

Goat (chèvre) cheese	4 oz.	113 g
Mango chutney, finely chopped	2 tbsp.	30 mL
Finely chopped fresh cilantro	1 tbsp.	15 mL
Finely chopped fresh mint	1 tbsp.	15 mL
Coarsely ground pepper	1/2 tsp.	2 mL
Pumpernickel cocktail bread slices	12	12
Thin mango slices	6	6

Combine first 5 ingredients until smooth.

Spread 1/3 of cheese mixture over 4 bread slices. Top with 4 bread slices and spread tops with another 1/3 of cheese mixture.

Trim mango slices to fit bread slices and arrange over cheese mixture. Spread remaining cheese mixture over remaining bread slices. Place, cheese side down, over mango. Spray both sides of sandwiches with cooking spray. Heat a large frying pan, greased with cooking spray, on medium. Add sandwiches and cook for 2 minutes per side until toasted. Cut sandwiches into halves and secure with cocktail picks. Makes 8 bites.

*1 **bite:** 90 Calories; 3.5 g Total Fat (0.5 g Mono, 0 g Poly, 2 g Sat); 5 mg Cholesterol; 11 g Carbohydrate (1 g Fibre, 4 g Sugar); 4 g Protein; 200 mg Sodium*

Edamame Purée on Sesame Squares

Wasabi-spiked edamame tops crisp wrappers with sesame seeds, promising a scintillating flavour experience. These squares can be made up to two days ahead; allow them to cool completely before storing them in an airtight container.

Spring roll wrappers (8 inch, 20 cm, square)	4	4
Egg white (large), fork-beaten	1	1
Black sesame seeds	2 tbsp.	30 mL
Sesame seeds	2 tbsp.	30 mL
Frozen shelled edamame	1 cup	250 mL
Lemon juice	2 tbsp.	30 mL
Mirin	2 tbsp.	30 mL
Grated lemon zest (see Tip, page 10)	1 tsp.	5 mL
Wasabi paste	1 tsp.	5 mL
Salt	1/4 tsp.	1 mL
Pepper	1/4 tsp.	1 mL

Spray 1 side of 2 wrappers with cooking spray and top each with 1 of remaining wrappers. Cut into 2 inch (5 cm) squares to make a total of 32 squares (see How To, below). Brush with egg white.

Combine sesame seeds and sprinkle over squares. Arrange on a greased baking sheet and bake in a 425°F (220°C) oven for 4 minutes until crisp and golden. Transfer to a wire rack and cool.

Cook edamame in boiling salted water for 5 minutes. Drain and rinse with cold water. Drain well. Transfer to a food processor.

Add remaining 6 ingredients and process until smooth. Spoon into a small freezer bag with small corner snipped off. Pipe onto sesame squares. Makes 32 squares.

1 square: 20 Calories; 0.5 g Total Fat (0 g Mono, 0 g Poly, 0 g Sat); 0 mg Cholesterol; 2 g Carbohydrate (0 g Fibre, 1 g Sugar); 1 g Protein; 35 mg Sodium

HOW TO CUT WRAPPERS
Layer the wrappers. Cut into squares.

Lemon Cream Puffs

Delicate pastries encase smooth lemon cream in these light-as-a-feather treats. You can make and fill the cream puffs in advance, but do not dust with icing sugar. Store them in the freezer in an airtight container for up to one month. Let stand at room temperature to thaw, dust with icing sugar and serve.

Milk	1/2 cup	125 mL
Butter	2 tbsp.	30 mL
Salt, sprinkle		
All-purpose flour	2/3 cup	150 mL
Large eggs	2	2
Whipping cream	1/2 cup	125 mL
Lemon curd	1/2 cup	125 mL
Grated lemon zest	1 tsp.	5 mL
Icing (confectioner's) sugar, sprinkle		

Bring first 3 ingredients to a boil in a small saucepan on medium-high, stirring occasionally. Reduce heat to medium.

Add flour and stir vigorously for 1 minute. Mixture will pull away from sides of pan to form a soft dough. Transfer dough to a medium bowl.

Add eggs, 1 at a time, beating well after each addition until well combined and dough is thick and glossy. Spoon dough into a piping bag fitted with a large star tip. Pipe twenty-four 1 1/2 inch (3.8 cm) rosettes, about 1 inch (2.5 cm) apart, onto a greased baking sheet. Bake in a 425°F (220°C) oven for 10 minutes until puffed. Reduce heat to 350°F (175°C) and bake for 10 minutes until golden and dry. Cool. Trim a 1/4 inch (6 mm) slice from top of each cream puff. Set tops aside.

Beat whipping cream until stiff peaks form. Fold in lemon curd and lemon zest. Spoon into a piping bag fitted with a large star tip and pipe onto cream puffs. Cover with tops. Sprinkle with icing sugar. Makes 24 cream puffs.

1 cream puff: 50 Calories; 33 g Total Fat (1 g Mono, 0 g Poly, 2 g Sat); 25 mg Cholesterol; 5 g Carbohydrate (0 g Fibre, 1 g Sugar); 1 g Protein; 20 mg Sodium

ABOUT LEMON CURD

Lemon curd is a thick spread made of egg yolks, sugar, butter and lemon juice. It makes a great alternative to jam or jelly on bread, scones and English muffins.

Orange Blossom Little Cakes

Delicately flavoured mini-cupcakes shyly steal the spotlight. The floral notes of the light orange blossom buttercream would be highlighted by a finishing touch of edible flowers.

All-purpose flour	1 cup	250 mL
Granulated sugar	1/2 cup	125 mL
Grated orange zest (see Tip, page 10)	1 1/2 tsp.	7 mL
Baking powder	1 tsp.	5 mL
Salt	1/8 tsp.	0.5 mL
Butter, cut up and softened	1/2 cup	125 mL
Large egg	1	1
Whipping cream	1/4 cup	60 mL
Orange juice	2 tbsp.	30 mL
Whipping cream	3/4 cup	175 mL
Instant vanilla pudding powder	2 tbsp.	30 mL
Orange blossom water	2 tsp.	10 mL

Edible flowers, as garnish

Combine first 5 ingredients. Add butter and beat until mixture is crumbly.

Combine next 3 ingredients and add to flour mixture. Beat for 1 minute until smooth. Line 24 mini-muffin cups with paper liners and fill with batter until 3/4 full. Bake in a 350°F (175°C) oven for 12 minutes until a wooden pick inserted in centre comes out clean. Let stand in pan for 10 minutes before removing to wire racks to cool.

Combine remaining 3 ingredients in a bowl and beat on high until stiff peaks form. Spoon into a small freezer bag with small corner snipped off and pipe icing onto cakes. Garnish with edible flowers. Makes 24 mini cupcakes.

1 mini cupcake: 100 Calories; 7 g Total Fat (2 g Mono, 0 g Poly, 4.5 g Sat); 30 mg Cholesterol; 9 g Carbohydrate (0 g Fibre, 4 g Sugar); 1 g Protein; 35 mg Sodium

ABOUT EDIBLE FLOWERS

Borage flowers make lovely edible garnishes, either fresh or crystallized. Be sure to remove the slightly prickly stems before using. Other edible flowers suitable for decorating sweets include pansies and violas. All three flowers are very easy to grow.

Chocolate Cherry Ice Cream Sandwiches

Everyone will fall in love with these inviting treats at first sight. Sinfully rich chocolate cookies sandwich sweet cherry ice cream for a fabulously fun grown-up delight.

All-purpose flour	1 cup	250 mL
Cocoa, sifted if lumpy	1/4 cup	60 mL
Salt	1/4 tsp.	1 mL
Butter, softened	6 tbsp.	90 mL
Granulated sugar	1/3 cup	75 mL
Large egg	1	1
Vanilla extract	1 tsp.	5 mL
Granulated sugar	4 tsp.	20 mL
Carton of chocolate cherry ice cream	1.5 qt.	1.5 L

Combine first 3 ingredients in a bowl.

Beat butter and sugar in a bowl until light and fluffy. Add egg and vanilla and beat until smooth. Add flour mixture and mix until no dry flour remains. Shape into a flattened disc. Roll out dough on a lightly floured surface to 1/4 inch (6 mm) thickness. Cut out circles using a lightly floured 2 inch (5 cm) cookie cutter. Roll out scraps to cut out more circles. Arrange circles 1 inch (2.5 cm) apart on greased cookie sheets.

Sprinkle with sugar and bake in a 350°F (175°C) oven for 8 minutes until firm. Let stand on cookie sheets for 5 minutes before removing to wire racks to cool. Makes about 28 cookies.

Remove carton from ice cream and cut ice cream into 3/4 inch (2 cm) thick slabs. Cut out 14 circles using a 2 inch (5 cm) cookie cutter. Place between 2 cookies. Freeze for at least 1 hour until ready to serve. Makes 14 ice cream sandwiches.

1 ice cream sandwich: 230 Calories; 11 g Total Fat (1.5 g Mono, 0 g Poly, 6 g Sat); 40 mg Cholesterol; 30 g Carbohydrate (1 g Fibre, 22 g Sugar); 4 g Protein; 95 mg Sodium

Mint and Melon Sparkler

The combination of fresh watermelon, lime and mint creates a light, refreshing treat perfect for sipping on a sunny afternoon on the patio. For a cool look, present this drink in tall, highball style glasses and garnish each glass with a wedge of watermelon; keep the rind on for extra colour.

Chopped seedless watermelon, chilled	6 cups	1.5 L
Lime juice	1/2 cup	125 mL
Granulated sugar	6 tbsp.	90 mL
Fresh mint leaves	24	24
Club soda, chilled	1/2 cup	125 mL

Process first 4 ingredients, in 2 batches, in a blender until smooth.

Using a sieve, strain mixture into a pitcher. Gently stir in club soda. Makes about 5 1/3 cups (1.35 L).

1 cup (125 mL): 110 Calories; 0 g Total Fat (0 g Mono, 0 g Poly, 0 g Sat); 0 mg Cholesterol; 29 g Carbohydrate (1 g Fibre, 25 g Sugar); 1 g Protein; 10 mg Sodium

ABOUT MINT

The mint family is large, diverse and well known, and some cuisines, such as those of North Africa and the Middle East, use it extensively. It's also been used as a medicine for millennia. Mint is easy to grow in containers, so you can plant a pot, set it in a partly shaded spot and snip some leaves into fruit salads all summer long. For variety, plant several different types in the same container.

Limon Spritzer

Dry white wine with a citrus twist—tart, refreshing sips under the evening sky will encourage mingling among your crowd. Use a sweeter wine such as a Gewürztraminer, or even a lemon-lime soft drink, if you prefer more sweetness. Do not make this recipe ahead or the bubbles will disappear.

26 oz. (750 mL) bottle of Riesling, chilled	1	1
Small lemon, thinly sliced, seeds removed, chilled	1	1
Small lime, thinly sliced, seeds removed, chilled	1	1
Club soda, chilled	3 cups	750 mL

Combine first 3 ingredients in a large pitcher. Using a wooden spoon, press or "muddle" lemon and lime slices.

Gently stir in club soda. Makes about 7 cups (1.75 L).

1 cup (250 mL): 90 Calories; 0 g Total Fat (0 g Mono, 0 g Poly, 0 g Sat); 0 mg Cholesterol; 5 g Carbohydrate (1 g Fibre, 1 g Sugar); 0 g Protein; 25 mg Sodium

ABOUT MUDDLING

When a recipe asks you to muddle ingredients, it means to use a wooden spoon or a "muddler" (a rod with a flat end), to mash or crush the ingredients.

Peach Mango Guacamole

Everyone is drawn to guacamole, with its vivid colour and fabulous flavour. This version, with a fresh fruit twist, won't disappoint—it's smooth and spicy with a hint of summery sweetness. Processing the onion and spices into a paste blends the flavours better and helps them mix into the avocado more smoothly.

Finely chopped red onion	1/2 cup	125 mL
Lime juice	6 tbsp.	90 mL
Chopped fresh cilantro	1/4 cup	60 mL
Finely chopped small red chili pepper (see Tip, page 146)	2 tsp.	10 mL
Salt	3/4 tsp.	4 mL
Smoked (sweet) paprika	1/2 tsp.	2 mL
Large avocados	4	4
Diced mango	3/4 cup	175 mL
Diced peeled peach (see Tip, below)	3/4 cup	175 mL

Process first 6 ingredients in a blender until smooth.

Coarsely mash avocado until chunky. Stir in mango, peach and onion mixture until combined. Makes about 4 cups (1 L).

1/3 cup (75 mL): 120 Calories; 10 g Total Fat (7 g Mono, 1 g Poly, 1.5 g Sat); 0 mg Cholesterol; 10 g Carbohydrate (5 g Fibre, 3 g Sugar); 2 g Protein; 150 mg Sodium

Tip: To peel peaches, dip them into a pot of boiling water for 30 seconds, then plunge them into a bowl of ice water. The skins will split and peel off easily.

ABOUT BUYING AVOCADOS

Avocado skins darken and the fruit goes soft when avocados are ripe. If you don't need them immediately, buy underripe avocados and allow them to ripen at room temperature for three to five days. If you need ripe ones right away, look for rinds that are nearly black and flesh that yields slightly to gentle pressure. If avocados are very soft, they are probably overripe and may be brown inside.

Corn Pancakes with Corn Salsa

Paired with a confetti-like corn salsa, these fun little cornmeal cakes have real personality—the fresh, savoury elements of cilantro and jalapeño balance with sweet bites of kernel corn. These pancakes are excellent paired with chicken, pork or steak.

Fresh kernel corn	2 cups	500 mL
Finely diced red onion	1 cup	250 mL
Finely diced red pepper	1 cup	250 mL
Lime juice	3 tbsp.	45 mL
Finely chopped jalapeño pepper	2 tbsp.	30 mL
(see Tip, page 146)		
Salt	1/4 tsp.	1 mL
Cooking oil	1 tsp.	5 mL
All-purpose flour	3/4 cup	175 mL
Yellow cornmeal	3/4 cup	175 mL
Chopped fresh cilantro	2 tbsp.	30 mL
Chili powder	1 tbsp.	15 mL
Granulated sugar	1 tbsp.	15 mL
Baking soda	1 tsp.	5 mL
Salt	1/2 tsp.	2 mL
Large egg	1	1
Buttermilk	1 cup	250 mL
Cooking oil	1 tbsp.	15 mL

Combine first 3 ingredients in a serving bowl. Reserve 1 cup (250 mL) in a small bowl. Add next 3 ingredients to corn mixture in serving bowl to make salsa. Toss and set aside.

Heat cooking oil in a frying pan on medium-high. Add reserved corn mixture and cook for 5 minutes until onion is softened and corn is browned. Remove from heat and let stand for 15 minutes.

Combine next 7 ingredients in a bowl. Add cooled corn mixture and stir.

Whisk remaining 3 ingredients and add to flour mixture. Stir until just combined. Using 2 tbsp. (30 mL) batter for each pancake, cook on a greased griddle on medium-high for 2 minutes per side until golden. Serve with salsa. Makes about 18 pancakes.

1 pancake with 2 tbsp. (30 mL) salsa: 90 Calories; 2 g Total Fat (1 g Mono, 0 g Poly, 0 g Sat); 15 mg Cholesterol; 16 g Carbohydrate (1 g Fibre, 2 g Sugar); 2 g Protein; 190 mg Sodium

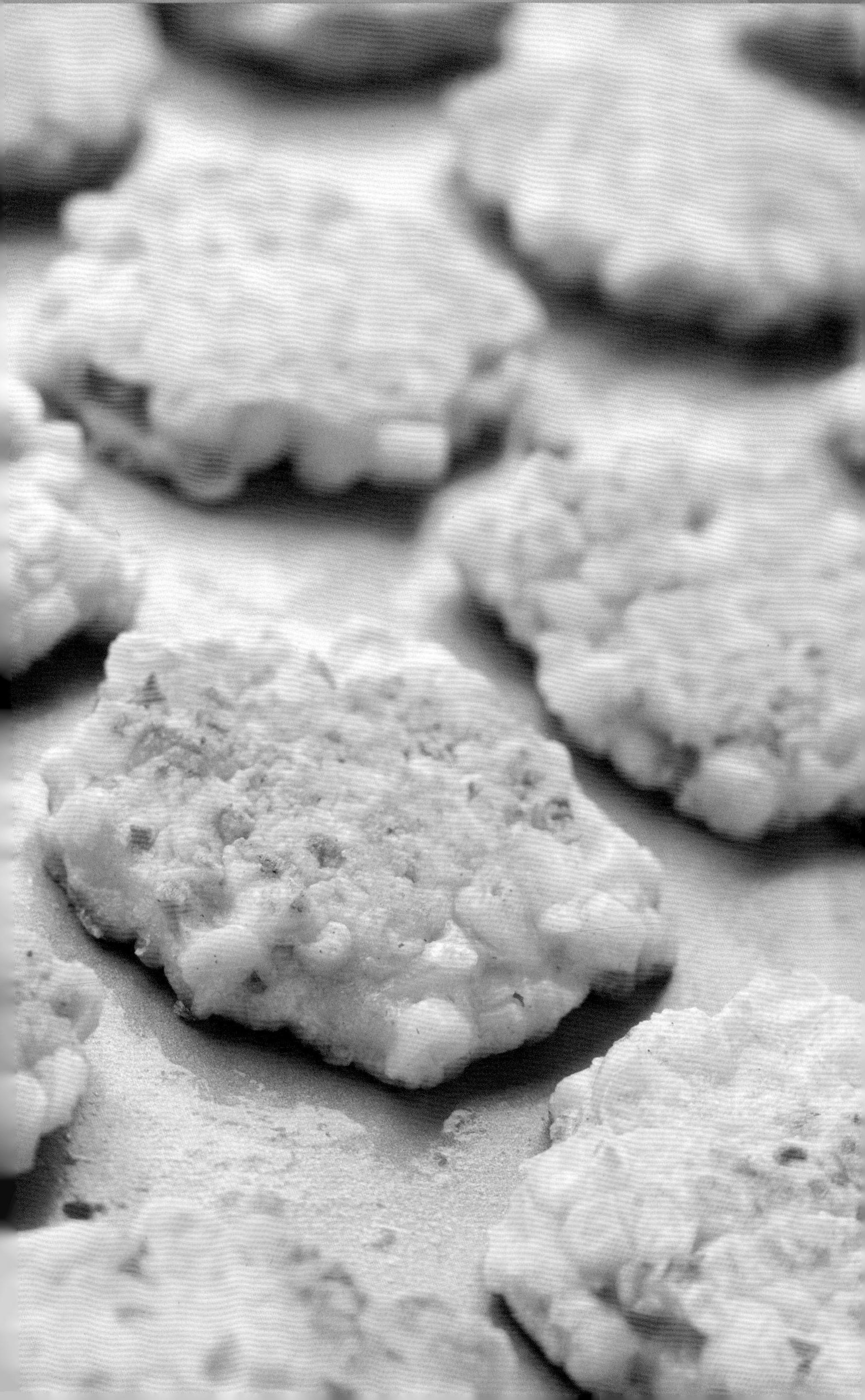

Smoky Shrimp Ceviche

This delightfully spicy ceviche is reason enough to start a party—the fun addition of popcorn and cilantro sprigs pushes it over the top.

Uncooked shrimp (peeled and deveined)	1 lb.	454 g
Diced seeded tomato	1 cup	250 mL
Finely diced red onion	1/4 cup	60 mL
Chopped fresh cilantro	3 tbsp.	45 mL
Finely chopped fresh chives	3 tbsp.	45 mL
Cooking oil	2 tsp.	10 mL
Chopped onion	1 cup	250 mL
Lime juice	1/4 cup	60 mL
Orange juice	1/4 cup	60 mL
Granulated sugar	1 tbsp.	15 mL
Finely chopped chipotle pepper in adobo sauce	2 tsp.	10 mL
Diced jalapeño pepper (see Tip, page 146)	1 tsp.	5 mL
Salt	1/4 tsp.	1 mL
Popped corn	1 1/2 cups	375 mL

Cook shrimp in boiling water until pink. Drain and cool in ice water for 10 minutes until cold. Drain well. Chop and transfer to a bowl.

Stir in next 4 ingredients.

Heat cooking oil in a frying pan on medium. Add onion and cook for 8 minutes until softened. Transfer to a blender or food processor.

Add next 6 ingredients and process until smooth. Pour over shrimp mixture and stir. Chill for 1 hour to blend flavours.

Spoon into 6 glasses and garnish with popcorn. Serve with remaining popcorn on the side. Serves 6.

1 serving: *140 Calories; 4.5 g Total Fat (1 g Mono, 1 g Poly, 0 g Sat); 115 mg Cholesterol; 11 g Carbohydrate (1 g Fibre, 5 g Sugar); 16 g Protein; 220 mg Sodium*

ABOUT CORN

Corn is believed to have originated in Mexico or Central America. The earliest traces of corn date back 7000 years, and there is much archeological evidence of its importance as a food crop to native peoples across the Americas. It was also used by indigenous peoples as currency, made into fuel, jewelry and construction material and even smoked. The existence of popcorn can be traced back 6000 years.

Crab Cakes on Corn Sauté with Papaya Mojo Sauce

Kick off your soirée with plated servings of appetizing crab cakes on a vibrant bed of corn and cherry tomatoes, drizzled with a wickedly fresh herbed papaya sauce.

Chopped papaya	1 cup	250 mL
Chopped fresh parsley	1/4 cup	60 mL
Olive oil	1/4 cup	60 mL
Chopped fresh cilantro	3 tbsp.	45 mL
Lime juice	3 tbsp.	45 mL
Small red chili pepper, chopped (see Tip, page 146)	1	1
Garlic clove, chopped	1	1
Salt	1/2 tsp.	2 mL
6 oz. (170 g) cans of crabmeat, squeezed dry	2	2
Fresh bread crumbs (see Tip, below)	3/4 cup	175 mL
Finely chopped celery	3 tbsp.	45 mL
Finely chopped green onion	3 tbsp.	45 mL
Mayonnaise	3 tbsp.	45 mL
Olive oil	1 tbsp.	15 mL
Olive oil	1 tsp.	5 mL
Fresh corn kernels	1 1/2 cups	375 mL
Finely diced yellow pepper	1 cup	250 mL
Finely diced red pepper	1 cup	250 mL
Salt	1/4 tsp.	1 mL
Pepper	1/4 tsp.	1 mL

Process first 8 ingredients in a blender or food processor and set aside.

Combine next 5 ingredients in a bowl. Shape into 8 cakes, about 1/2 inch (12 mm) thick. Chill, covered, for 30 minutes. Heat 1 tbsp. (15 mL) of olive oil in a large frying pan on medium. Cook cakes for 4 minutes per side until browned. Transfer to a plate and cover to keep warm.

Add second amount of olive oil to pan. Add corn and cook for 5 minutes until browned. Add remaining 4 ingredients and stir for 1 minute. Transfer to 4 serving plates, top with crab cakes and drizzle with papaya sauce. Serves 4.

1 serving: 490 Calories; 29 g Total Fat (18 g Mono, 5 g Poly, 4 g Sat); 75 mg Cholesterol; 37 g Carbohydrate (5 g Fibre, 8 g Sugar); 23 g Protein; 940 mg Sodium

ABOUT MOJO SAUCE

A sauce popular in Caribbean countries, mojo (mo-ho) is most closely
associated with the Canary Islands and Cuba. It's often served with bread at
the beginning of a meal, and is used in Cuba to marinate pork. Athough mojo
may be flavoured with a variety of ingredients, such as lemon, orange or lime
juice, vinegar, tomato, pepper and avocado, the basic recipe for this sauce
contains garlic, olive oil and cumin or paprika.

Churrasco con Chimichurri

There's something enticing about meaty sirloin skewers, with their bold look and even bolder flavour—especially when perfectly grilled with an aromatic herb chimichuri. Make the chimichurri no more than four hours ahead or the vibrant colour will fade.

Fresh parsley leaves, lightly packed	1 cup	250 mL
Cooking oil	1/2 cup	125 mL
Fresh oregano leaves, lightly packed	1/2 cup	125 mL
Chopped shallots	1/4 cup	60 mL
Red wine vinegar	1/4 cup	60 mL
Garlic cloves, chopped	6	6
Granulated sugar	1 tbsp.	15 mL
Salt	1 1/2 tsp.	7 mL
Pepper	1/2 tsp.	2 mL
Cayenne pepper	1/4 tsp.	1 mL
Beef top sirloin roast, cut into 1 1/2 inch (3.8 cm) cubes	1 1/2 lbs.	680 g
Metal skewers (12 inches, 30 cm, each)	4	4

Process first 10 ingredients in a food processor or blender until herbs are finely chopped. Reserve half of parsley mixture and chill until needed.

Combine beef and remaining parsley mixture in a large resealable freezer bag. Chill for 4 hours.

Thread beef onto skewers. Discard marinade. Cook skewers on a greased grill on medium for 5 minutes, turning once, until medium-rare or beef reaches desired doneness. Let stand, tented with foil, for 5 minutes. Spoon reserved parsley mixture over skewers and serve with a squeeze of lemon. Makes 4 skewers.

1 serving: 670 Calories; 42 g Total Fat (23 g Mono, 8 g Poly, 8 g Sat); 85 mg Cholesterol; 18 g Carbohydrate (5 g Fibre, 4 g Sugar); 34 g Protein; 990 mg Sodium

ABOUT CHIMICHURRI AND CHURRASCO

Chimichurri is a garlicky sauce originating in Argentina. It usually accompanies grilled meats or is used as a meat marinade. Churrasco is a Spanish and Portugese term referring to different cuts of beef or to grilled meats in general.

Caribbean Cornish Hens

Golden-roasted Cornish hens are infused with sweet curry, jerk seasoning and unexpected spices—bright garnishes and a bed of greens set the scene for a true celebration.

Chopped green onion	1/2 cup	125 mL
Cooking oil	3 tbsp.	45 mL
Brown sugar, packed	1 tbsp.	15 mL
Lime juice	1 tbsp.	15 mL
Hot curry paste	2 tsp.	10 mL
Jerk seasoning paste	1 tsp.	5 mL
Salt	3/4 tsp.	4 mL
Pepper	1/2 tsp.	2 mL
Butter, melted	1 tbsp.	15 mL
Cornish game hens (1 – 1 1/2 lbs., 454 – 680 g, each)	2	2
Mixed greens, lightly packed	2 cups	500 mL
Lime slices, for garnish		
Small red chili peppers, for garnish		
Sprigs of thyme, for garnish		

Process first 8 ingredients in a blender or food processor until almost smooth.

Combine melted butter and 1 tbsp. (15 mL) of onion mixture in a small cup.

Rub remaining onion mixture under skin of hens and over all surfaces Chill, covered, for 2 hours. Tie legs to tail. Place hens on a greased baking sheet and cook on centre rack in a 375°F (190°C) oven for 25 minutes, brushing twice with butter mixture, until internal temperature reads 180°F (82°C). Let stand, tented with foil, for 10 minutes. Serve on a bed of mixed greens, garnished with lime slices, chili peppers and thyme. Serves 4.

1 serving: 480 Calories; 37 g Total Fat (17 g Mono, 7 g Poly, 9 g Sat); 175 mg Cholesterol; 5 g Carbohydrate (1 g Fibre, 4 g Sugar); 29 g Protein; 600 mg Sodium

ABOUT CORNISH GAME HENS

Despite their name, these hens are not from Cornwall and are not game birds. They originated in the U.S., and were specifically developed by poultry producers to get a small chicken with mostly white meat. Their name is derived in part from one of the types of hens used to breed them.

Broiled Snapper with Tropical Salsa

Sunny and light, yet big on flavour, spice-speckled snapper pairs with bright, juicy salsa and crisp tortillas in this vibrant dish.

Diced mango	3/4 cup	175 mL
Diced papaya	3/4 cup	175 mL
Diced fresh pineapple	3/4 cup	175 mL
Diced seeded Roma tomato	3/4 cup	175 mL
Diced English cucumber	1/2 cup	125 mL
Diced red onion	1/2 cup	125 mL
Chopped fresh cilantro	1/4 cup	60 mL
Lime juice	1/4 cup	60 mL
Chopped jalapeño pepper, (see Tip, page 146)	3 tbsp.	45 mL
Hot pepper sauce	3/4 tsp.	4 mL
Salt	1/4 tsp.	1 mL
Flour tortillas (9 inch, 23 cm, diameter)	2	2
Melted butter	2 tbsp.	30 mL
Salt	1/4 tsp.	1 mL
Cayenne pepper	1/8 tsp.	0.5 mL
Ground allspice	1/8 tsp.	0.5 mL
Red snapper fillets (about 5 oz., 140 g, each)	4	4

Combine first 11 ingredients and let stand for 1 hour.

Spray tortillas with cooking spray. Cut each into 10 wedges and arrange on an ungreased baking sheet. Bake in a 350°F (175°C) oven for 15 minutes until crisp.

Combine next 4 ingredients and brush over both sides of fillets. Arrange on a greased baking sheet and broil on top rack in oven for 2 minutes per side until fish flakes easily with a fork. Serve with salsa and tortilla chips. Serves 4.

1 serving: 380 Calories; 11 g Total Fat (3.5 g Mono, 1.5 g Poly, 4.5 g Sat); 70 mg Cholesterol; 37 g Carbohydrate (4 g Fibre, 10 g Sugar); 33 g Protein; 570 mg Sodium

ABOUT PAPAYA

Papaya is often used in marinades because it contains the enzyme papain, which helps to tenderize meat. For this reason, if you're using it in a fruit salad, add it just before serving or it may soften the other fruits. Ripe papaya is delicious scooped and eaten directly from the shell. In tropical countries, green papaya is used as a vegetable in savoury dishes.

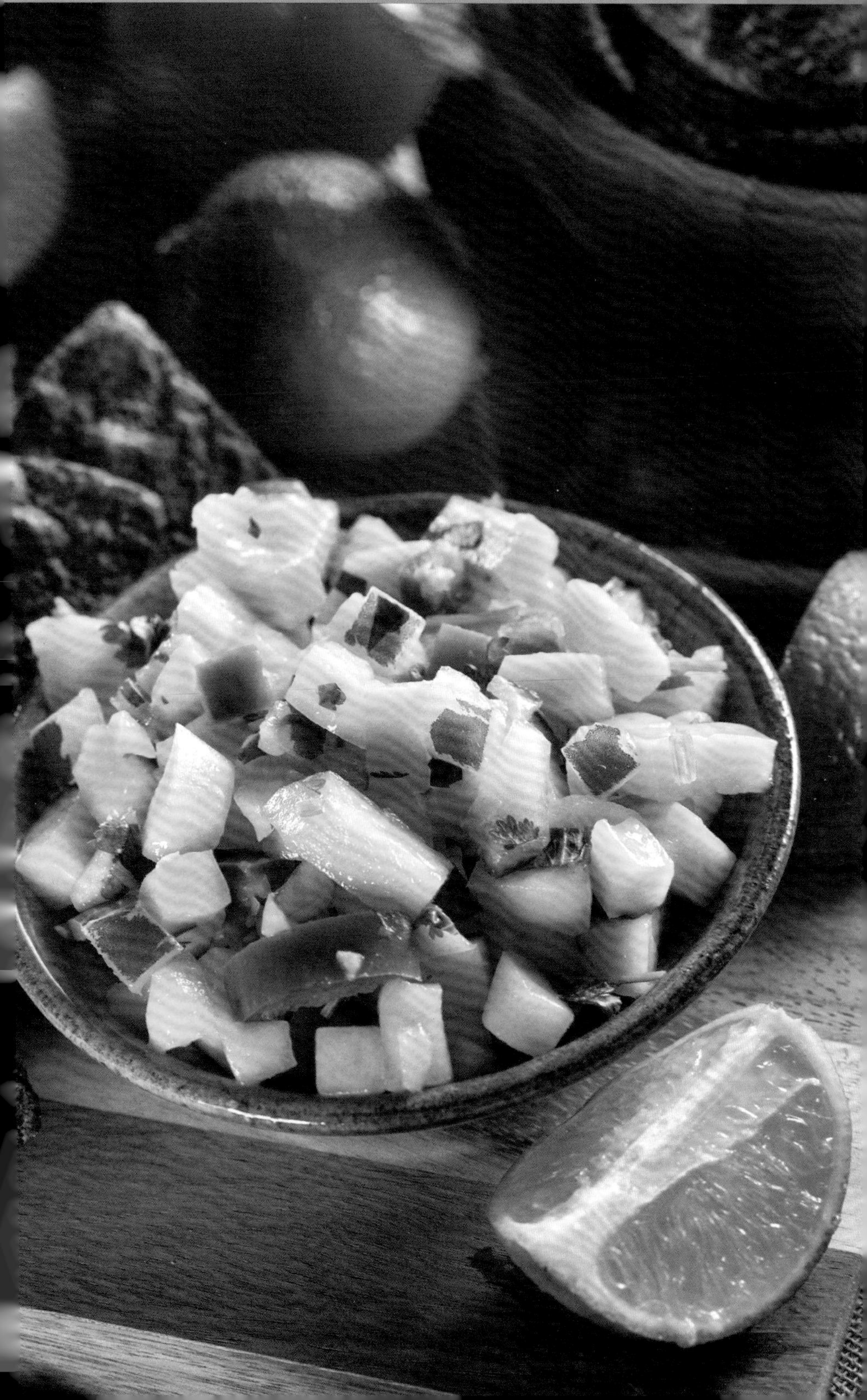

Black Bean and Rice Salad

Fun, festive and fresh—this intense rice and bean blend packs some heat, and injects colourful texture into a fiesta-style spread.

Cooked long-grain white rice	3 cups	750 mL
19 oz. (540 mL) can of black beans, rinsed and drained	1	1
Chopped arugula, lightly packed	1 cup	250 mL
Diced red pepper	1 cup	250 mL
Finely diced red onion	1/2 cup	125 mL
Fresh kernal corn	1/2 cup	125 mL
Finely diced jalapeño pepper (see Tip, below)	3 tbsp.	45 mL
Red wine vinegar	1/4 cup	60 mL
Olive oil	3 tbsp.	45 mL
Brown sugar, packed	1 tbsp.	15 mL
Jerk seasoning paste	2 tsp.	10 mL
Garlic clove, chopped	1	1
Lime juice	1 tsp.	5 mL
Ground allspice	1/4 tsp.	1 mL
Chopped fresh basil	2 tbsp.	30 mL
Chopped fresh cilantro	2 tbsp.	30 mL
Chopped fresh parsley	1 tbsp.	15 mL

Combine first 7 ingredients in a large serving bowl.

Process next 7 ingredients in a blender until smooth. Add remaining 3 ingredients and process until combined. Drizzle over rice mixture and stir. Makes about 7 cups (1.75 L).

1/2 cup (125 mL): 120 Calories; 3 g Total Fat (2 g Mono, 0 g Poly, 0 g Sat); 0 mg Cholesterol; 19 g Carbohydrate (2 g Fibre, 2 g Sugar); 4 g Protein; 85 mg Sodium

Tip: Hot peppers contain capsaicin in the seeds and ribs. Removing the seeds and ribs will reduce the heat. Wear rubber gloves when handling hot peppers and avoid touching your eyes. Wash your hands well afterwards.

Sparkling Lime Jicama Slaw

Crunchy, sweet jicama and apple contrast with orange slices and spicy radish, all dressed in bold, tangy vinaigrette—a bright-tasting slaw to pair with grilled entrées.

Lime juice	1/4 cup	60 mL
Cooking oil	3 tbsp.	45 mL
Granulated sugar	4 tsp.	20 mL
Chili paste (sambal oelek)	1 tsp.	5 mL
Salt	3/4 tsp.	4 mL
Grated lime zest (see Tip, page 10)	1/2 tsp.	2 mL
Julienned jicama	4 cups	1 L
Small orange segments, halved	2 cups	500 mL
Thinly sliced tart apple (such as Granny Smith), see How To, below	1 cup	250 mL
Thinly sliced radish	3/4 cup	175 mL
Thinly sliced red onion, chopped	1/4 cup	60 mL
Finely chopped fresh mint	3 tbsp.	45 mL

Whisk first 6 ingredients until sugar is dissolved.

Add remaining 6 ingredients and toss. Makes about 7 cups (1.75 L).

1/2 cup (125 mL): 60 Calories; 3 g Total Fat (2 g Mono, 1 g Poly, 0 g Sat); 0 mg Cholesterol; 9 g Carbohydrate (3 g Fibre, 5 g Sugar); trace Protein; 140 mg Sodium

HOW TO SLICE AN APPLE

To thinly slice an apple, cut four sides from the apple, almost to the core. Lay the pieces flat side down and thinly slice lengthwise. Discard the apple core.

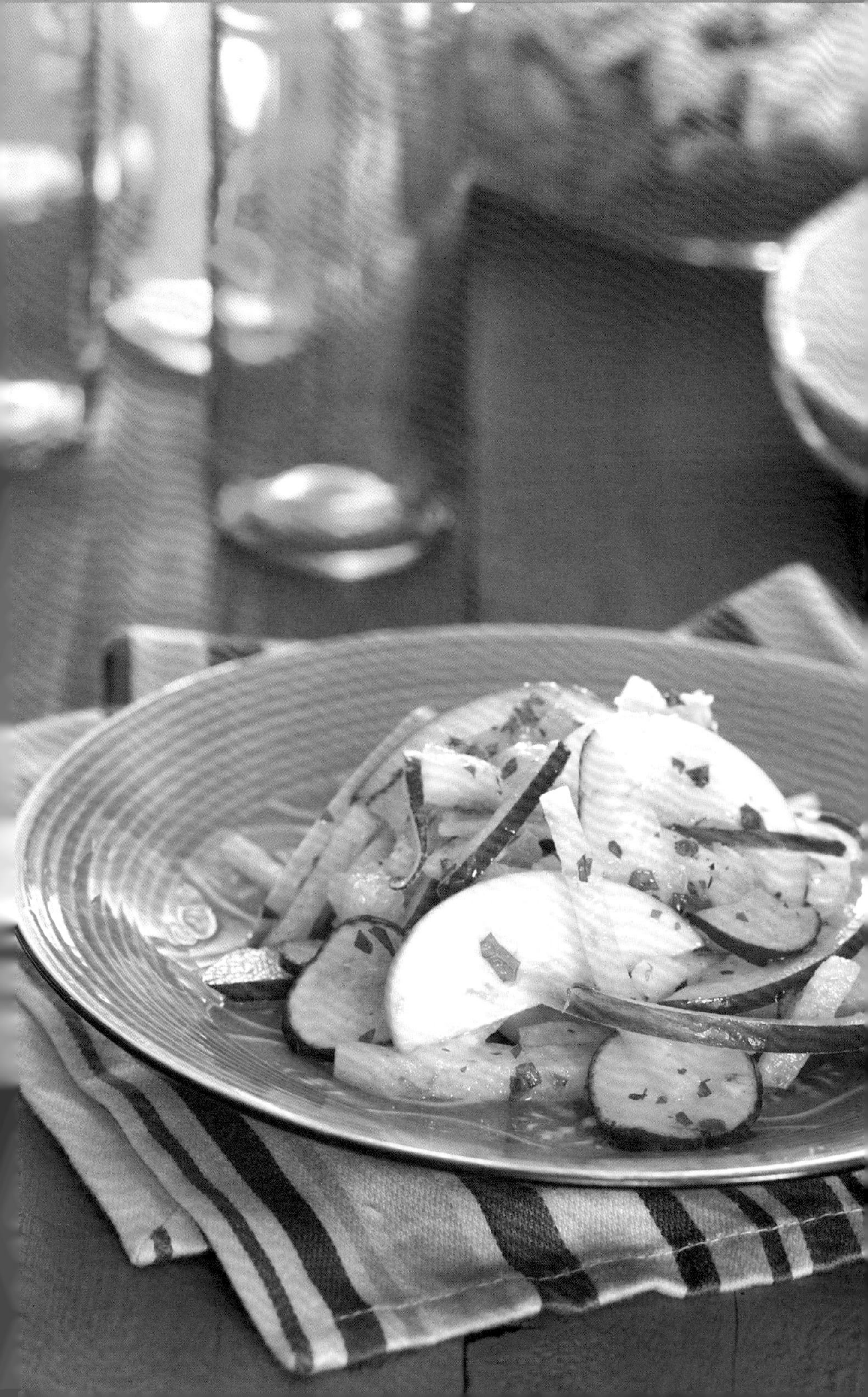

Key Lime Mousse

This light, silky-smooth mousse is tart, yet sweet, infused with fabulous key lime.

Unflavoured gelatin	1 tsp.	5 mL
Water	2 tbsp.	30 mL
Egg yolks, large	3	3
Granulated sugar	1/2 cup	125 mL
Key lime juice	1/2 cup	125 mL
Grated key lime zest (see Tip, page 10)	1 tsp.	5 mL
Butter, cut up	1/4 cup	60 mL
Whipping cream	1 cup	250 mL
Shaved chocolate, for garnish		

Sprinkle gelatin over water in a small bowl.

Whisk next 4 ingredients in a saucepan on medium until combined. Add butter and stir for 5 minutes until just starting to simmer but not boil. Remove from heat. Stir in gelatin mixture until dissolved. Transfer to a bowl and place plastic wrap directly on surface of lime mixture. Chill for 1 hour, stirring twice, until cooled and just starting to thicken.

Beat whipping cream until stiff peaks form. Fold 1/3 of whipped cream into lime mixture until almost combined. Fold in remaining whipped cream. Chill, covered, for 1 hour. Stir before spooning into serving glasses. Garnish with shaved chocolate. Makes about 2 1/2 cups (625 mL).

1/2 cup (125 mL): 340 Calories; 27 g Total Fat (8 g Mono, 1 g Poly, 16 g Sat); 205 mg Cholesterol; 25 g Carbohydrate (0 g Fibre, 21 g Sugar); 3 g Protein; 25 mg Sodium

ABOUT KEY LIMES

Key limes grow in the Florida Keys and are smaller, rounder and a little yellower than the regular limes found at the supermarket. At one time they were hard to find, but in recent years availability has improved, so you may find them sold in small mesh bags at your local grocery store. Because Key limes are small, try using a garlic press to juice them. The tiny limes fit perfectly into the press.

Caribbean Gin Fizz

Fizzy gin with a summery citrus twist—a refreshing and airy drink perfect for cooling sips to follow spicy fare.

Coconut milk	1/3 cup	75 mL
Gin	1/3 cup	75 mL
Eggnog liqueur (such as Advocaat)	1/4 cup	60 mL
Lime juice	1/4 cup	60 mL
Simple syrup (see How To, below)	3 tbsp.	45 mL
Orange blossom water	1 tsp.	5 mL
Ice cubes	2 cups	500 mL
Club soda	1 1/3 cups	325 mL

Put first 6 ingredients into a cocktail shaker.

Add ice cubes and shake vigorously until blended. Strain into 4 tall glasses.

Slowly stir in club soda. Serves 4.

1 serving: 140 Calories; 4 g Total Fat (0 g Mono, 0 g Poly, 3.5 g Sat); 0 mg Cholesterol; 8 g Carbohydrate (0 g Fibre, 6 g Sugar); 0 g Protein; 20 mg Sodium

HOW TO MAKE SIMPLE SYRUP

Make simple syrup by dissolving two parts sugar into one part boiling water. Once cool, it is ready to use. Any remaining syrup can be refrigerated indefinitely.

ABOUT ORANGE BLOSSOM WATER

Orange blossom water is a fragrant distillation of bitter-orange blossoms. It's used to flavour baked goods, drinks and savoury dishes. Bitter oranges are also known as Seville oranges.

Summer Pudding

Fresh-picked saskatoons are the stars of this berry pudding, positively saturated with colour and flavour. Garnish with the prettiest berries you've got for an elegant touch.

Fresh saskatoon berries	3 cups	750 mL
Sliced fresh strawberries	2 cups	500 mL
Fresh blackberries	1 1/2 cups	375 mL
Frozen raspberry juice concentrate	1/3 cup	75 mL
Granulated sugar	3 tbsp.	45 mL
Lemon juice	2 tbsp.	30 mL
Stale egg bread slices (see Tip, below)	18	18
Whipping cream	1/2 cup	125 mL
Granulated sugar	2 tsp.	10 mL

Bring first 5 ingredients to a boil in a saucepan. Reduce heat to medium and simmer for 5 minutes, stirring occasionally, until sugar is dissolved and berries release juices.

Stir in lemon juice and cool. Drain fruit, reserving juices. Line six 6 oz. (170 mL) round ramekins with plastic wrap, leaving overhanging sides. Place on a baking sheet with sides.

Using a 3 inch (7.5 cm) round cookie cutter, cut 18 bread rounds. Dip 6 rounds into fruit juice and place in bottoms of ramekins. Top with about 3 tbsp. (45 mL) of berry mixture. Repeat layers, ending with bread on top. Bread may be above tops of ramekins. Drizzle with any remaining berry juice. Bring plastic wrap over bread and place another layer of plastic wrap over ramekins. Place a second baking sheet on top of ramekins. Place several heavy cans on top of baking sheet and chill overnight. Some juices may seep out during chilling.

Unmold puddings onto serving plates. Beat whipping cream and sugar until soft peaks form. Serve with puddings. Serves 6.

1 serving: 540 Calories; 14 g Total Fat (4.5 g Mono, 2 g Poly, 6 g Sat); 85 mg Cholesterol; 92 g Carbohydrate (10 g Fibre, 16 g Sugar); 14 g Protein; 600 mg Sodium

Tip: In this pudding, stale bread works better than fresh for soaking up juices to create the desired texture. If you don't have stale bread handy, leave fresh slices out for several hours until they are dry to the touch but still somewhat pliable.

Petite Vanilla Peach Pavlovas

Vanilla bean heightens the flavour of fresh peaches atop glossy white meringue, while a sweet coulis adds depth. The meringue shells can be made one day ahead and stored in an airtight container in a cool, dry place.

Egg whites (large), room temperature	4	4
Cream of tartar	1 tsp.	5 mL
Granulated sugar	1 cup	250 mL
Sliced fresh peaches	3 cups	750 mL
Granulated sugar	2 tbsp.	30 mL
Vanilla extract	1 tsp.	5 mL
Whipping cream	1 cup	250 mL
Granulated sugar	2 tbsp.	30 mL
Vanilla bean, split	1/2	1/2
Sour cream	1/2 cup	125 mL
Peach jam	1/2 cup	125 mL
Apple juice	1 tbsp.	15 mL
Lemon juice	1 tbsp.	15 mL

Trace six 3 inch (7.5 cm) circles, 2 inches (5 cm) apart, on a sheet of parchment paper. Turn over and place on a baking sheet. Beat egg whites and cream of tartar in a large bowl until soft peaks form. Add sugar, 1 tbsp. (15 mL) at a time, beating constantly until stiff peaks form. Fill piping bag fitted with a large star tip. Pipe spirals onto parchment to fill circles. Pipe a ring on edge of each circle to form a shell. Bake on the centre rack in a 225°F (110°C) oven for 45 minutes until dry to the touch but still white. Turn off oven and let stand in oven for 2 to 3 hours until cooled completely.

Combine next 3 ingredients and let stand for 1 hour.

Combine whipping cream and remaining sugar in a large bowl. Scrape seeds from vanilla bean into bowl. Beat until stiff peaks form. Fold in sour cream.

Process remaining 3 ingredients in a blender until smooth. Place meringues on 6 serving plates. Spoon whipped cream mixture into meringues. Top with peach slices and dollop with remaining whipped cream mixture. Spoon peach jam mixture onto plates. Serves 6.

1 serving: 430 Calories; 17 g Total Fat (4.5 g Mono, 0.5 g Poly, 10 g Sat); 55 mg Cholesterol; 70 g Carbohydrate (2 g Fibre, 65 g Sugar); 5 g Protein; 60 mg Sodium

ABOUT PAVLOVA

Pavlova, made of crisp meringue filled with whipped cream and fruit, is a lovely, light dessert perfectly suited for summertime. Pavlova originated in Australia and is named for the famous Russian ballerina Anna Pavlova.

Raspberry Basil Panna Cotta

Who wouldn't be delighted to set eyes on these silky smooth panna cottas? Tart raspberries contrast delightfully with their texture and bold colour. Serve with port or a sparkling Shiraz to complement the savoury basil flavour.

Unflavoured gelatin	2 tsp.	10 mL
Milk	1/4 cup	60 mL
Whipping cream	1 cup	250 mL
Milk	2/3 cup	150 mL
Granulated sugar	1/2 cup	125 mL
Vanilla extract	1 tsp.	5 mL
Fresh basil leaves	2	2

Sprinkle gelatin over milk and let stand for 1 minute.

Heat next 5 ingredients in a saucepan on medium, stirring occasionally, until boiling. Remove from heat and discard basil. Stir in gelatin mixture until dissolved. Pour through a fine mesh sieve into a liquid measure. Pour into six 4 oz. (170 mL) ramekins and chill, covered, overnight. Makes 6 panna cottas.

1 panna cotta: 210 Calories; 13 g Total Fat (35 g Mono, 0 g Poly, 8 g Sat); 50 mg Cholesterol; 21 g Carbohydrate (0 g Fibre, 20 g Sugar); 3 g Protein; 45 mg Sodium

ABOUT FRESH BASIL

Fresh basil is widely available, especially during the summer months, and is much more aromatic and flavourful than the dried version. Choose fresh basil that is evenly coloured and not wilted. Wrap it in damp paper towels, seal it in a plastic bag and refrigerate for up to four days.

Rustic Cheese Tart

A seductive offering on a warm summer evening. Cheesy pastry is sprinkled with fresh dill, the very essence of summer. Paired with seedless red grapes and a glass of wine, it's an upscale indulgence. Try your hand at pairing different cheeses with the feta in this recipe. Use Cheddar, Monterey Jack or havarti— anything goes, as long as it's a melting cheese that complements feta.

Grated four-cheese blend	1/2 cup	125 mL
Crumbled feta cheese	1/3 cup	75 mL
Egg yolk (large)	1	1
14 oz. (397 g) package of puff pastry, thawed according to package directions	1/2	1/2
Large egg	1	1
Water	1 tbsp.	15 mL
Finely chopped fresh dill	1 tbsp.	15 mL

Combine first 3 ingredients in a bowl.

Roll out pastry on a lightly floured surface to a 10 x 12 inch (25 x 30 cm) rectangle. Place on an ungreased baking sheet. Combine egg and water and brush over pastry. Scatter cheese mixture over top, leaving a 1 inch (2.5 cm) border on all sides. Bake on centre rack in a 425°F (220°C) oven for 20 minutes until golden and puffed.

Sprinkle with dill and let stand on a wire rack for 10 minutes. Cut into quarters. Cut each quarter into thin wedges and arrange on a serving plate. Cuts into 16 wedges.

1 wedge: 100 Calories; 7 g Total Fat (3 g Mono, 0.5 g Poly, 2.5 g Sat); 35 mg Cholesterol; 6 g Carbohydrate (0 g Fibre, 0 g Sugar); 3 g Protein; 110 mg Sodium

Cheese and Fruit with Spiced Honey

A wonderfully fragrant honey is drizzled over the small, delicate bites on this appetizing platter.

Liquid honey	1/3 cup	75 mL
Apple brandy (such as Calvados)	2 tbsp.	30 mL
Sprig of thyme	1	1
Star anise	1	1
Vanilla bean, split lengthwise	1/2	1/2
Fresh figs, stems trimmed, halved lengthwise	8	8
Granulated sugar	2 tbsp.	30 mL
Applewood-smoked Cheddar cheese	4 oz.	113 g
Brie cheese round	4 oz.	113 g
Pistachios, toasted	30	30
Fresh raspberries	30	30

Combine honey and brandy in a saucepan. Add next 3 ingredients and bring to a boil. Remove from heat and let stand, covered, until cool. Discard solids and set mixture aside.

Sprinkle cut sides of figs with sugar. Heat a non-stick frying pan on medium. Cook figs, sugar side down, for 5 minutes until sugar is melted.

Place Cheddar and brie on a large serving platter. Arrange figs around cheese.

Put pistachios inside raspberries. Scatter over platter and drizzle with honey mixture. Serves 4.

1 serving: 460 Calories; 20 g Total Fat (3.5 g Mono, 1 g Poly, 11 g Sat); 45 mg Cholesterol; 75 g Carbohydrate (5 g Fibre, 49 g Sugar); 15 g Protein; 340 mg Sodium

ABOUT FIGS

Because they are highly perishable, figs are often dried or preserved—so take advantage of fresh figs while they are in season, which is generally from mid- to late-summer through to early autumn. Regardless of variety, figs have soft flesh and contain many tiny seeds. Look for plump and tender (but not mushy) figs with firm stems, and enjoy within a couple days of purchasing.

Chocolate Strawberry Semifreddo

Who doesn't love chocolate and strawberries? Please your guests with this sweet and tangy confection filled with summer-fresh strawberries and milk chocolate bits.

Finely chopped fresh strawberries, drained	2 cups	500 mL
Balsamic vinegar	1 tbsp.	15 mL
Large eggs	2	2
Egg yolk (large)	1	1
Granulated sugar	1/2 cup	125 mL
Milk chocolate bars (3 1/2 oz., 100 g each), melted	2	2
Whipping cream	1 1/4 cups	300 mL

Line a 9 x 5 inch (23 x 12.5 cm) loaf pan with plastic wrap. Toss strawberries with balsamic vinegar and set aside.

Beat eggs, egg yolk and sugar in a medium stainless steel bowl. Set over simmering water in a large saucepan so that bottom of bowl is not touching water. Beat constantly for 5 minutes until mixture is thickened and fluffy. Remove from heat.

Gently fold in chocolate and let stand for 10 minutes.

Beat whipping cream until soft peaks form. Gently fold in chocolate mixture until combined. Fold in strawberry mixture. Pour into prepared loaf pan and freeze, covered, overnight. Let stand for 10 minutes before serving. Makes about 5 cups (1.25 L).

1/3 cup (75 mL): 180 Calories; 11 g Total Fat (4 g Mono, 0 g Poly, 6 g Sat); 70 mg Cholesterol; 17 g Carbohydrate (1 g Fibre, 15 g Sugar); 3 g Protein; 25 mg Sodium

Iced Chaiccino

This silky-smooth iced chai goes down easy. A sweet and creamy concoction with a bit of floral spice—just like a warm summer night. Be sure to use skim milk because it froths up better in the blender than full-fat milk.

Skim milk	**1 cup**	**250 mL**
Sweetened chai tea concentrate, chilled	**2 cups**	**500 mL**
Half-and-half cream	**1 cup**	**250 mL**
Brown sugar, packed	**1 tbsp.**	**15 mL**
Vanilla extract	**1 tsp.**	**5 mL**
Ice cubes		
Ground cardamom, sprinkle		

Process milk in a blender until frothy. Transfer to a bowl and let stand for 5 minutes. Using a large spoon to hold back froth, pour milk back into blender.

Add next 4 ingredients to blender and process until combined.

Pour over ice cubes in 4 glasses and spoon froth over top. Sprinkle with cardamom. Makes about 4 1/2 cups (1.1 L).

1 cup (250 mL): 130 Calories; 6 g Total Fat (2 g Mono, 0 g Poly, 4 g Sat); 20 mg Cholesterol; 15 g Carbohydrate (0 g Fibre, 12 g Sugar); 3 g Protein; 60 mg Sodium

ABOUT CHAI TEA CONCENTRATE

Liquid chai concentrate is a spiced, tea-based syrup which is combined with milk or water to create chai-flavoured beverages. The convenience factor of chai concentrate has made it very popular, and it is often used by coffee franchises to make hot and chilled chai beverages.

Honeydew Lemon Grass Granita

This gorgeously green granita is the ultimate in refreshment. A hint of lemon grass adds dimension and a sophisticated flavour.

Coarsely chopped honeydew	4 1/2 cups	1.1 L
Water	1 cup	250 mL
Granulated sugar	1/2 cup	125 mL
Lemon grass, bulbs only, chopped	2	2

Process honeydew in a food processor until smooth.

Heat and stir remaining 3 ingredients in a saucepan on medium until sugar is dissolved (see Tip, below). Bring to a boil. Reduce heat to medium-low and simmer, covered, for 5 minutes. Strain into a bowl and discard lemon grass. Stir in honeydew and pour into a 9 x 13 inch (23 x 33 cm) pan. Freeze, covered, for 1 hour. Rake top of mixture with a fork and freeze for another hour. Repeat every hour for 3 hours until set. Makes about 6 cups (1.5 L).

1/3 cup (75 mL): 40 Calories; 0 g Total Fat (0 g Mono, 0 g Poly, 0 g Sat); 0 mg Cholesterol; 10 g Carbohydrate (0 g Fibre, 9 g Sugar); 0 g Protein; 10 mg Sodium

Tip: Make sure the sugar is completely dissolved before the solution is brought to a boil or else it will crystallize.

ABOUT LEMON GRASS

Lemon grass shares an essential oil, citral, with lemons, giving it a refreshing, sour, lemony flavour. Store lemon grass stalks tightly wrapped in the refrigerator for up to two weeks.

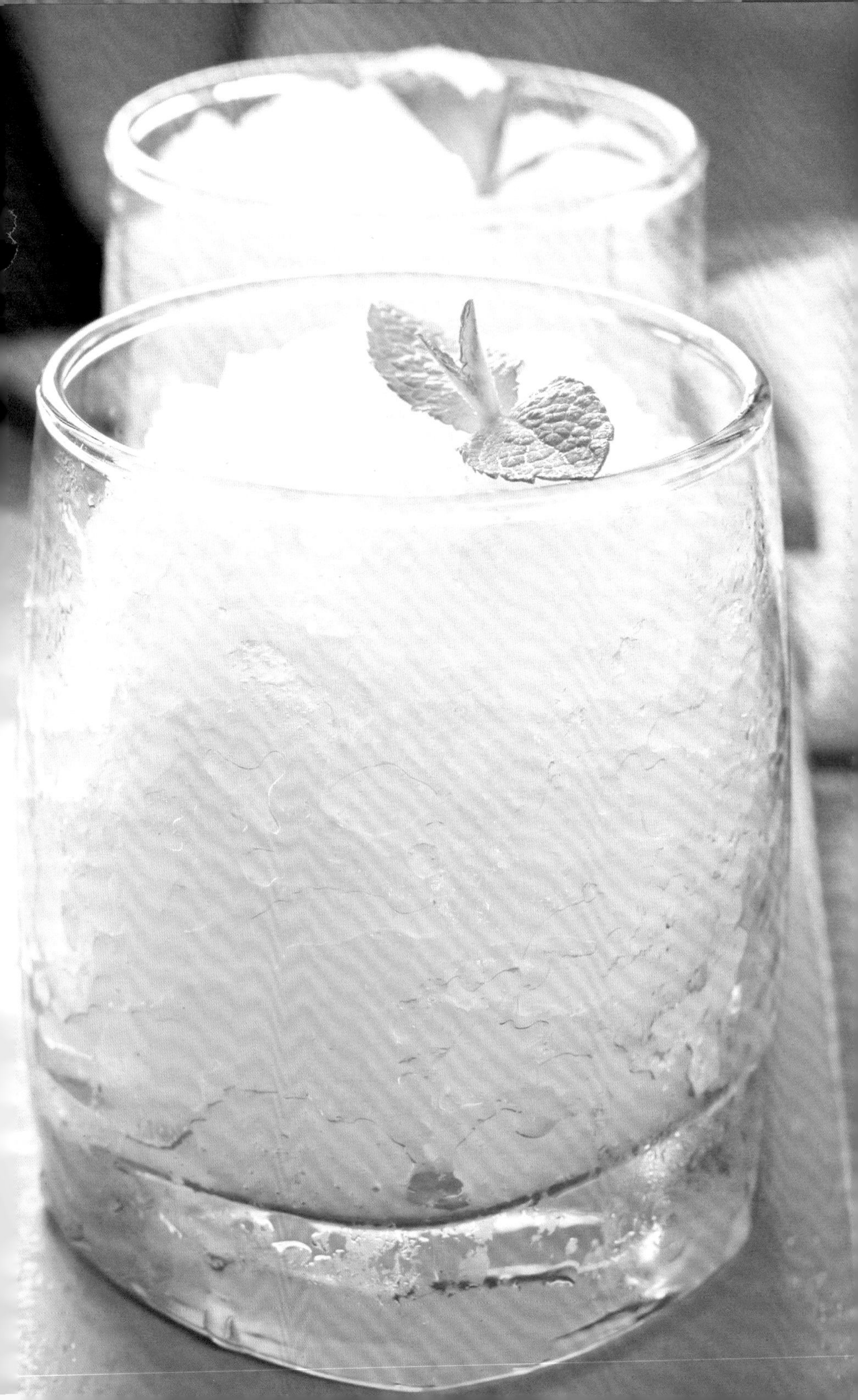

Lounging Lantern Martini

Slow the night down with smooth, sweet sips of this sophisticated martini.

Fresh raspberries	12	12
Cocktail picks	4	4
Hazelnut liqueur (such as Frangelico)	1/2 cup	125 mL
Grappa	1/3 cup	75 mL
Orange liqueur (such as Grand Marnier)	1/4 cup	60 mL
Ice cubes		
Raspberry liqueur (such as Chambord)	1/4 cup	60 mL

Thread 3 raspberries on each cocktail pick. Place 1 pick in each martini glasses.

Combine next 3 ingredients in a cocktail shaker. Add ice cubes and shake vigorously until blended. Slowly strain into martini glasses.

Slowly drizzle 1 tbsp. (15 mL) raspberry liqueur against inside of each martini glass. Makes 4 martinis.

1 martini: 170 Calories; 0 g Total Fat (0 g Mono, 0 g Poly, 0 g Sat); 0 mg Cholesterol; trace Carbohydrate (0 g Fibre, 0 g Sugar); 0 g Protein; 0 mg Sodium

HOW TO DRIZZLE LIQUEUR INTO GLASS

Pour the raspberry liqueur slowly against the inside of each martini glass so that it layers beneath the other liquid. It has a higher specific gravity than the other ingredients, and will therefore sink to the bottom.

Lemonade

Combine 2 cups (500 mL) boiling water, 3/4 cup (175 mL) granulated sugar and 1/4 tsp. (1 mL) grated lemon zest in a large heatproof bowl until sugar is dissolved. Stir in 2 cups (500 mL) cold water and 1 cup (250 mL) lemon juice. Serve over ice in tall glasses with lemon slices for garnish. Makes about 5 1/2 cups (1.4 L).

Mint Julep Lemonade

Using a wooden spoon, crush or "muddle" 30 fresh mint leaves, 2 tbsp. (30 mL) orange liqueur (such as Triple Sec) and 1 tsp. (5 mL) granulated sugar in a 2 quart (2 L) pitcher. Add 4 cups (1 L) lemonade and 2/3 cup (150 mL) bourbon whiskey (such as Jim Beam). Stir well. Pour over ice into rocks glasses. Makes about 5 cups (1.25 L).

Cherry Pink Lemonade Pops

Process 2 cups (500 mL) lemonade, 1 1/2 cups (375 mL) pitted fresh cherries, 1/2 cup (125 mL) plain yogurt and 1 tbsp. (5 mL) grenadine syrup in a blender until smooth. Fill 6 paper cups 3/4 full. Cover each cup with plastic wrap, and poke a freezer pop stick through the centre of the wrap. Freeze for at least 6 hours or overnight until firm. To loosen, run the bottom of each cup under hot water for 3 to 4 seconds. Makes 6 pops.

Basil Lemon Grass Lemonade

Using a wooden spoon, crush or "muddle" 10 fresh basil leaves, 2 tbsp. (30 mL) chopped ginger root, 2 tbsp. (30 mL) chopped lemon grass bulb, 2 lime quarters, 1 tsp. (5 mL) granulated sugar and 1/2 small red chili pepper in a cocktail shaker. Add 2 tbsp (30 mL) vodka and 1 cup (250 mL) lemonade. Fill shaker with ice and replace lid. Hold firmly and shake vigorously. Strain through sieve over ice into short glass. Garnish with a lemongrass stalk, a basil sprig and a twist of lime. Makes about 1 1/3 cups (325 mL).

Ginger Herb Lemonade

Combine 1/2 cup (125 mL) lemonade, 1/4 cup (60 mL) ginger ale, 2 tbsp. (30 mL) Pimm's No. 1, 4 fresh mint leaves, 2 thin orange slices and 2 thin English cucumber slices in a cocktail shaker. Add ice. Shake vigorously. Pour into tall cocktail glass. Garnish with fresh cherries. Makes about 1 1/2 cups (375 mL).

St. Clements Lemonade

Pour 1/2 cup (125 mL) orange juice, 1/4 cup (60 mL) lemonade, 1/4 cup (60 mL) tonic water and 2 tsp. (10 mL) lime juice over ice in a tall glass. Stir. Garnish with orange and lime slices. Makes about 1 cup (250 mL).

Raspberry Iced Tea Lemonade

Place 4 raspberry herbal tea bags into an 8 cup (2 L) pitcher. Pour 3 cups (750 mL) boiling water over top. Stir. Let stand for 5 minutes. Remove and discard tea bags. Allow tea to cool, then stir in 3 cups (750 mL) lemonade. Pour over ice into tall glasses. Makes 6 cups (1.5 L).

Apricot Lemonade Bellini

Combine 2 tbsp. (30 mL) chilled apricot nectar and 2 tbsp. (30 mL) chilled lemonade in a tall champagne flute. Slowly pour 1/2 cup (125 mL) chilled sparkling white wine (such as Prosecco) over top. Makes about 3/4 cup (175 mL).

INDEX